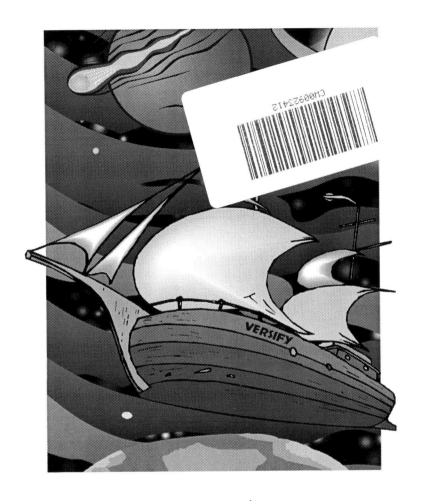

POETIC VOYAGES CHESHIRE

Edited by Lucy Jeacock

First published in Great Britain in 2001 by
YOUNG WRITERS
Remus House,
Coltsfoot Drive,
Peterborough, PE2 9JX
Telephone (01733) 890066

HB ISBN 0 75433 232 2
SB ISBN 0 75433 233 0

FOREWORD

Young Writers was established in 1991 with the aim to promote creative writing in children, to make reading and writing poetry fun.

This year once again, proved to be a tremendous success with over 88,000 entries received nationwide.

The Poetic Voyages competition has shown us the high standard of work and effort that children are capable of today. It is a reflection of the teaching skills in schools, the enthusiasm and creativity they have injected into their pupils shines clearly within this anthology.

The task of selecting poems was therefore a difficult one but nevertheless, an enjoyable experience. We hope you are as pleased with the final selection in *Poetic Voyages Cheshire* as we are.

CONTENTS

Pownall Hall School

Rainow Primary School

Rushton CE Primary School

St Augustine's RC Primary School, Runcorn

St Basil's Primary School, Widnes

The Poems

MUMMY

When I was a little girl
Mummy used to say;
'Wash your hands before dinner
To rinse the germs away.'
That's just what I did,
The water went everywhere
Mummy shouted loud,
But, I didn't really care!
When I was a junior
Mummy did tell me;
'You've put too much make-up on,
You look so silly!'
I stamped up to her bedroom
Put lipstick on the wall!
Saying I'm not pretty,
Just isn't fair at all!
When I was a teenager,
Mummy made me cry
Because I had a boyfriend
He was a really lovely guy
She said I couldn't see him
I had to get her back
I washed away her champagne
From the expensive wine rack!
After all the arguments
Mummy is my mate,
She can be annoying
But, honestly she's great!

Marissa Pepper

IF COLOURS WERE ALIVE

If colours were alive,
What would they say?
What would they play and do each day?

Would yellow be happy,
Red be angry,
Blue be sad,
Green always envy?

Would yellow sing,
Red shout,
Blue cry,
Green muck about?

If colours were alive,
I know what they'd say,
I know what they'd play and do each day.
They would be normal,
Not red, blue, yellow or green,
They would have their own personalities,
Happy, sad, kind or mean.

Katherine Eaton

THE GREAT DOGS OF THE NORTH

The great dogs of the north, hear their cries,
Not far from where the dead deer lies.
Hunting by day or hunting by night,
Their speed gives even the snowshoe hares a fright.
Then down past the river where the salmon dive,
But danger lies ahead where the brown bears thrive.
The caribou flee, the pack on their tail,
Easily brought down is a beast, these dogs never fail.

Julia Nicholson (10)

Sit!

The sun did not shine
It was too wet to play
So we sat in the house
All that cold, cold wet day.

I sat there with Sally
We sat there we two
And I said, 'How I wish
We had something to do!'

Too wet to go out
And too cold to play ball
So we sat in the house
We did nothing at all.

So all we could do was to
Sit
  Sit
    Sit
      Sit
And we did not like it not one little bit
                      bit
                       bit
                        bit.

Kirsty Louise Gilmore (11)

LIFE

All the time people groan
and all day long they moan
they have good times
and they have smug times
some are fun
but some are glum
some people are stubborn
and some have been tolerant
some people are happy and try, try, try
but some people are unhappy and cry, cry, cry.

Vincent Goodall

MONSTER

The monster is a-coming,
He's coming down the street,
The monster is a-coming,
Guess who he's going to eat?
The monster is a-roaring,
He's roaring for his food,
The monster is a-roaring,
He's very rude!
The monster is a-jumping,
He's being such a clown,
The monster is a-jumping,
The roof is coming down!
He throws his food,
The waiter's hurt,
The monster shouts,
'Chef, you're dessert!'

George Morriss (10)
Bickerton CE Primary School

THE OCEAN

Shells and fishes, dolphins too,
Stand by the ocean just me and you,
Listen to the shell, it sounds like the sea,
Stand together, you and me
See the dolphins sing and play
The sea is so blue and calm today.
They leap and jump in the air
Then dive in the sea with such care.

The tide changes around
As the waves lash and pound
In cracks in the rocks
Pools we play with our nets
Picking up crabs,
I find two and sometimes three
They try desperately to hide from me
Shells and fishes, dolphins too,
Stand by the ocean just me and you.

Melissa Robertson (10)
Bickerton CE Primary School

WINTER'S COMING

On a track old trees snap
Close your eyes, wait and see,
No one else but you and me.
What do you hear?
Can you hear wind howling
Or maybe birds singing
Or leaves rustling
Now winter is here -
But there's nothing to fear.

Jessica Moyle (11)
Bickerton CE Primary School

Pizza

Sizzle, sizzle, spice, spice and all things nice.
Watch that pizza, it looks yum, so crispy and thin,
Just enough to fill my tum.
Sizzle, sizzle, spice, spice and all things nice.
Large or small, take your pick, it's your call,
There's no trick.
Sizzle, sizzle, spice, spice and all things nice.
Mozzarella cheese or pepperoni meat.
Sizzle, sizzle, spice, spice and all things nice.
Crispy base with tomato sauce.
Sizzle, sizzle, spice, spice and all things nice.
Lovely round and neat, no room left for another course.
Sizzle, sizzle, spice, spice and all things nice.
Sizzle, sizzle, spice, spice and all things nice.

Natalie Stevenson (10)
Bickerton CE Primary School

The Surprise

Early in the morning on a winter's day,
I heard something whimpering away,
I went to the bathroom to have a quick wash,
And when I had finished I looked quite posh,
I went downstairs and opened the door,
And there on the floor were seven tiny pups.
I didn't understand at first
But then it came quite clear
My dog had given birth to seven little puppies.
Eight weeks past of looking after seven puppies
But then the time had come to sell them away,
I was so sad and forlorn
But then I thought at least I have still got my lovely dog.

Michael Langton (11)
Bickerton CE Primary School

AUTOMOBILE

It's a four wheel automobile!
200 miles an hour, full power.
It's a road runner, it's a stunner!
Bright red in colour, oh how I love her!

It's a four wheel automobile!
Soft top, alloy wheels.
Rear spoiler, doesn't need a boiler!
It's a GTO, just watch her go!

It's a four wheel automobile!
Leather seating, music beating!
Goes like a rocket doesn't need a socket.
She's so fine, I wish she was mine!

James Lloyd (11)
Bickerton CE Primary School

THANK YOU J K

Harry Potter, what a book,
At those pages I must look.
Reading all about Harry,
Ron Weasley and Hermione.
You always know if you read on
Potter's gang will be having fun.
Out of bounds, breaking rules,
Trouble making, but they're no fools.
Turning the pages, the plot emerges,
Exciting adventures, witchcraft and curses.
Reading a book was never such fun,
        J K Rowling - well done!

Sam Green (9)
Bickerton CE Primary School

EATING THE UNIVERSE

One day I ate the universe
And put the big bang into reverse.
I swallowed all of those shiny stars
As well as Earth and bright red Mars.
And the best thing that I ate that day
Was the rich and creamy Milky Way.
I nearly got hit by Orion's arrow
As I ate that plough-like wheelbarrow.
But I wasn't having that much fun
When I burnt my hand on the fiery sun.
I thought I might have gone too far
When I gobbled up the huge Dog Star.
And I think that Mum got quite annoyed
When I ate up a huge asteroid.
Some aliens came to join me for dinner
And we made the galaxy so much thinner.
I ate the moon with its dust and dirt
Then I ate Neptune for dessert.
And by the time the clock struck one
The planets and the stars were all gone.

Christy Gowers (10)
Bickerton CE Primary School

A LIMERICK

There was a young man from Dubai,
Who really thought he could fly.
He bought a balloon
To float to the moon,
But the sand in his eyes made him cry.

Luke Ducker (9)
Bickerton CE Primary School

THE VOLCANO

Boiling lava, shooting, splashing,
Molten rock is thudding, crashing!

Disaster getting nearer, nearer
Explosions signal the end of an era.

Hot lava flows stream on and on,
The victims know it's all gone wrong.

Their houses lie as crumpled stones,
The molten rock crushes their bones.

The dreaded moment's now occurred,
The people's screams will not be heard.

And now the earth's colossal crust,
Is covered o'er with ash and dust.

Michael Conner (10)
Bickerton CE Primary School

THE MISSION

T he time has come to say goodbye
H igh above the Earth I'll fly.
E very thought on my exciting task

M any people with questions to ask.
O ver the hills and the clouds and the snow,
O pen the throttle and away I'll go.
N ext stop the moon, wow what a show.

Matthew Wild (11)
Bickerton CE Primary School

ART

Think of many things to paint,
Colours bold and colours faint,
Think of hills and trees and water blue,
Orange, yellow, purple too.
All the time in the world to spend,
If nothing begins, then nothing ends.

I dip my brush into the water,
Shake it dry, and start all over,
As I paint, my hand runs wild.
It spins around like an excited child.
All the time in the world to spend,
If nothing begins, then nothing ends.

My watercolour picture begins to take shape,
The splashes of colour drenching the paper,
While above my head, a stormy cloud,
Lightning bright, thunder loud.
All the time in the world to spend,
If nothing begins, then nothing ends.

Suddenly, water from the sky,
Ruins my picture, oh dear, oh my!
I hurry under a tree for shelter,
But that seems to make it worse, not better.
No more time in the world to spend,
Something began, but sadly, it ended.

Hannah Mumby (10)
Bickerton CE Primary School

MY PETS

I have a spotty doggy.
And Benjamin is his name.
He likes to go for walks
Each day in sun or wind or rain.
When I get his lead out
To take him up the hill
He jumps and bounces in the air
As it gives him such a thrill.

I have two pretty kitties
One's tabby, one's white.
They stay in the house in daytime
And go chasing bunnies at night.

Natalie Fraser (11)
Bickerton CE Primary School

MY CAT

My cat is curled up at night
Crouched up like a cake
In front of the fire,
I can't hear a sound
Nor a peak.

A gloomy glow
Catches his eye
And then cold
Light flashes back at him,
And then he ponders
Like a roaring tiger
In the middle of the night.

Kim Derricutt (10)
Bickerton CE Primary School

SNOW AROUND THE WORLD

The snow came in the night
And we woke to a world that was white
With glistening curvy soft trees
All sunk to their knees
The animals jumped in delight

The endless blue sky
With its crisp winter sun
Was showing the day had only begun
With excitement and laughter
We had breakfast, then after
We went up in the hills sledging for fun.

Jack Freeman (11)
Bickerton CE Primary School

WHAT WILL YOU DO?

There are people downstairs
What will you do?
You can jump out of the window
Or go to the loo.
Your family are all asleep
Come on please don't weep.
You can hide under the cover
Or pretend to be asleep
Although it probably is a creep.
When you wake up in the morning
You realise your dog is roaring
So you go back to bed
And find that you are dead.

Aydan Jones
Castle View Primary School

THE GLOOM

The rain is falling from the sky
The trees mope, the wind howls
And in a dark room far away from life
Gloom closes in on you.
'Whoosh' shouts the angry wind
'Splash' moans the sloshing rain
'Bang' screams the raging thunder
'Moan and groan' says the worst of them all, gloom.

People in the streets with umbrellas create a sea of blackness
People in the streets cover themselves with hats and scarves
To prevent the frosty wind hitting their faces.
There is no colour left in the world,
England is like a black and white movie
Soon the great warrior summer will fight gloom
But until then we live under its rule!

Tarrin Kennaway (11)
Castle View Primary School

THE SPEEDY CHEETAH

The cheetah is the fastest runner,
Stronger than the stunner.
To start with
Its teeth are as sharp as kitchen knives
Able to chop hives.
Pouncing on its prey
For a 10kg tray
It creeps to its den, hating all men,
Then chomps it down with a slurp,
Burp!

Keiron Cosgrove (10)
Castle View Primary School

BIRD

Little beak,
Flapping wings,
Tiny toes,
Long legs,
Feathery coat,
Bang! Bang!
The poor thing's dead.

Barry Wilkinson (11)
Castle View Primary School

DREAMS

Fly up in the sky
Fly with the birds and magpies
Fly above the trees
Fly above the cities
Dreams where you've never been before.

Sarah Marie Egan (11)
Castle View Primary School

SILLY SAUSAGES

Silly sausages sizzle like mad,
With tattoos which make them look bad.
They wear stupid shades looking so cool,
They're not even scared of a ghoul.
The jackets they wear are really weird,
Some of them have a hairy beard.

Vinny Atanasov (10)
Castle View Primary School

CANDLE

A flame flickers as the wind goes past
Yellow, orange, blue.

It floats freely as I run fast
Yellow, orange, blue.

The beam around the candle light
Yellow, orange, blue.

The flame holds on with all its might
Yellow, orange, blue.

It fades away when I am down the street,
Yellow, orange, blue.

A candle light, what a treat
Yellow . . . Orange . . . Blue . . .

Jessica Ayuya (11)
Castle View Primary School

CATS

Cats, cats everywhere,
In the cellar, up the stair.
Cats are playful, cats are great
So come on now everybody,
Let's celebrate.
Dance with your cats,
Dance with your cats,
Let's have fun and dance
With your cats.

Kimberley Halpin (10)
Castle View Primary School

GUNSHOT MIST

Lame hooves thumping, slowly banging,
Last of the swords quietly clanging,
Frightened voices, screaming, screeching
Over the bridge, loudly creaking.
All the people quickly rushing,
Running through the village, pushing.
Bodies falling, fading, dying,
Orphaned children, weeping, crying.
Everyone is madly famished,
All the houses have been damaged.

Grass is fading under horses' moves,
Whips flying and thundering hooves.
Mountains wearing from rock to mud,
Thrashing feet stop dead with a thud.
A bugle calls from far away,
The bright sun shines with colours gay.
The gushing of the water streaming,
In the gunshot mist it's gleaming.

Emma Jones (10)
Davenham CE Primary School

THE SPRING

Bulbs are being planted
The ice is clearing up
Snowmen are melting
Ready for the up

Weather is changing
We're going out to play
Spring is here
Hip hip hooray!

Adele Gee (10)
Davenham CE Primary School

THE WASHING MACHINE MAN

Early in the morning
Bubbling away
The washing machine man
Comes out to play.

He eats up all the powder
Then conditioner too
He tangles all the washing
Then rinses it through

He munches on some socks
Which he likes the best
When he's clean and satisfied
He loses interest

The cycle comes to an end
It's been a hectic day
The washing machine man needs a rest
Before more washing comes his way!

Harry Woodrow (9)
Davenham CE Primary School

PIZZA

Pizza, you're a yummy food
Round, fat and scrumptious.

I eat you for lunch and tea
It's the best, as you can see.

My favourite is tomato and cheese
I sometimes eat you with chips and peas.

Rosie Hilditch (9)
Davenham CE Primary School

BOOKS AND PENCILS

The loud and echoing school bell rings,
The children grab their bags and things,
The teachers are left all on their own,
In the air there's an eerie tone.

They're ready for a night out on the streets!
They tidy up and push in all the seats,
The teachers have finished, there is no more,
They say goodbye and lock the door.

The pencils and rubbers are scattered around,
All of a sudden there becomes a sound.
The pencils stand up and the rubbers join in,
The chalks break out of their biscuit tin.

The scissors break into the paper drawer,
The glue is sticking things to the floor,
The pencil sharpenings jump out of the bin,
All this catastrophe is hard to take in.

In the morning when the teacher comes in,
She sees the messy and tipped over bin.
So when you're asleep, cuddled up in bed
Just think what's happening at school instead.

Amy Clarke (11)
Davenham CE Primary School

PINK

I have a pink nightie
I have a pink chair
I have a pink dressing gown
And loads of pink things to wear.

I have a pink bed
I have a pink bear
I have pink fluffy slippers
And a pink rabbit right over there!

Stacy Anne Hancock (8)
Davenham CE Primary School

DUNGEON KEEPER

At home I have a computer game
It drives me round the bend
You can say I'm addicted to it
I try to do ten levels in the end

You have got to fight your enemies
And build your dungeon big
Attract your own little creatures
And make your workers dig

Give your vampires graveyards
Give your flies a lair
Train your animals wisely
And treat them with care

The enemies are the heroes
Who fight you till you're dead
And if you're lucky you won't die
But they will instead

This game is called Dungeon Keeper
And that's the way it will stay
Be kind to your creatures
And you might get your own way!

Sarah Capper (9)
Davenham CE Primary School

THE LIFE OF MY CATS MAUI AND ZUMA

I have two cats called Maui and Zuma
They have a completely different day
Zuma goes outside and acts like a puma
While Maui stays inside and sleeps.

Maui eats, sleeps, eat and sleep, eat and sleep
She steals Zuma's food
But Zuma doesn't say a peep
Zuma's the quiet one.

Zuma's wild in the day
But calm in the evening.
Maui's nickname is little May
She can say her name,

Maui sings her morning hymns
To wake up everyone in the morning.
Zuma's a ballerina, stretches her limbs,
Then runs to the cat-flap, demanding to go out.

I love my talented cats!

Kate Trevor (9)
Davenham CE Primary School

TELEVISION

Television is really great
And is very fun to watch with your mate
We relax on the sofa and open the sweets
We turn on the telly, we're in for a treat.

The soaps EastEnders and Coronation Street
My mum likes watching Cold Feet
Drama and comedy of all sorts
Football and all the other sports.

BBC1 and BBC2
Lots of channels just for you
Channel 4 and Channel 5
Some programmes are recorded, some are live.

Amy Burbidge (10)
Davenham CE Primary School

MOODS OF THE SEA

As the night draws on,
And the waves grow high,
I stand staring out of my window,
And see evil faces appear in the waves,
Then they crash down never to be seen again,
I close the curtains,
And close my eyes and dream . . .

Dream of the people who get caught in the waves,
Who perish in the swirling mass,
Dream of the people who float to safety,
And those less fortunate, the ones I pity.
I wake next morning,
And lie relaxed and think . . .

Think again of yesterday,
How the moods affected me,
But now, there's no sound at all,
Only children laughing and splashing,
I look out of the window,
And smile to myself.
The night is over now,
It's time for happiness again.

Nicola Weale (10)
Davenham CE Primary School

THE FARM

I live on a farm,
It's got a barn
For milking the cows
And keeping the ploughs.

Farmer Joe ploughs the fields
With tractors that have big wheels,
Eight chickens peck at their seed,
It's their favourite kind of feed.

Our deaf old dog called Nell
Manages to guard the farm well
But she chases the sheep
When they're trying to sleep!

Hannah Mitchell (9)
Davenham CE Primary School

SEASHORE

The seashore in the summer
Sunny and bright
People sunbathing near the sea
Colourful umbrellas for the shade
Children swimming, making sandcastles
Building the sand
Bigger than pets
Bigger than the sky
Getting dark
Everyone going back to their hotels
Pretty lights glowing in the harbour.

Stephanie Smith (7)
Davenham CE Primary School

BLUE

The sky is so blue,
Like deep, deep in the ocean,
The fish are so pretty too,
All colours like a rainbow.

My friend has blue eyes
They sparkle like a firework
In the dark, blue night,
Going on forever like us two.

The moon glows,
In the dark, blue night,
The stars twinkle,
Like a diamond ring.

The sun shines,
In the light blue sky,
All the brightness,
Shining down on me.

George McCoy (9)
Davenham CE Primary School

FLOWERS IN THE SUN

Red flowers, green flowers,
Blue flowers as well.
They all are bright
And have a lovely smell
When you're up in the sky so high
You can see the flowers below, when you're passing by.

Rachel Newson (7)
Davenham CE Primary School

THE LADY OF THE SEA

A figure staggered towards the sea;
Waves ferociously crashing,
Foam spraying and hissing;
The wind howling angrily.

Misty shadows swept around;
Making not a single sound.
A swish of a long black cloak,
Brushing the dark cold waves.

The sea's vexation continued ugly,
Tearing everything apart,
The figure plunged into total darkness,
Not to be seen by any man.

The sea hissed to its resentment
Not to join a calm contentment
Lightning illuminated in the sky
The end of a wonderful beauty.

Emily Dignum (11)
Davenham CE Primary School

SCHOOL

I slam the car door and run through the gate,
I rush to the classroom and oh no I'm late.
The square root of twenty, where've you've been
Oh I thought I could come in and not be seen.
It's twenty past nine you've done it again,
Now sit down and write this, but I've lost my pen
School's nearly over, it's time to go home,
I slam the car door run through the gate,
I rush to the classroom and oh no I'm late . . .

Stephanie Rough (10)
Davenham CE Primary School

CATS

Cats can be small
Cats can be tall.
Cats can be fat
Cats can sit on mats.
Some cats are fluffy
Others can be scruffy.
Cats can be prowlers
Cats can be growlers.
Some cats are sugar white
And some cats are very bright.
Cats can be dozy
Cats can be cosy.
Cats can be clean
Cats can be mean.
Cats can bounce
And cats can pounce.
Cats can play
Cats can sit in the sun all day.
Cats can be tatty
Cats can be scatty.
Cats can be crazy
Cats can be lazy.
Cats can wear coats
Cats can sail on boats.
Cats can be hissing
Cats can be missing.
Cats can be rough
Cats can be tough.
Cats can be mad
Cats can be bad.

Nicola Booth (10)
Dean Row Community Junior School

SCULLY

I am short and furry,
And I lie by the fire,
I love to be pampered,
As much as I desire.

I purr when I'm happy,
And hiss when I'm not,
My favourite food is Whiskers in jelly,
I love it a lot!

I scratch at the carpet,
To sharpen my claws,
I climb up the curtains,
And run round the walls.

When out in the garden,
I chase all the birds,
I try to play fair,
But it just doesn't work!

My owners are tall,
And a very strange lot,
Maybe they're aliens,
Maybe they're not.

Can you guess where I am?
I'm lying on the mat,
Can you guess what I am?
I'm a short furry cat!

Kasey Boswell (10)
Dean Row Community Junior School

AN ENTRANCE TO THE WORLD

Beyond a television screen
Lies a world of much serene
Roam the rapids!
Search the skies!
Venture further!
Make the pies!
Hear the stories!
Read the books!
Run the race!
Improve your looks!
Join the heroes!
Drive the car!
Swim with sharks!
Adventure far!
So the saying 'couch potato',
Is it really true?
Books or television?
It's entirely up to you!

Phillippa Oakes (11)
Dean Row Community Junior School

THE LARGE ELEPHANT

The large elephant
Weighs a ton
Grey, large, slow,
Like a huge boulder sitting there
Grey like the dark night sky
Like an ant that no one notices
The large elephant
Reminds us how big animals can be.

Tom Emmons (11)
Dean Row Community Junior School

WHO'S THERE?

Who's there
Sitting by the shore
All alone on a rock
Combing her long hair?

Who's there
Sitting very still
With noone else around
Watching the still sea?

Who's there
In the darkness of the night
Underneath the moonlight
Sitting very quietly?

Who's there
Sitting by the shore
All alone on a rock
Combing her long hair?

Who's there?

Siobhan Way (11)
Dean Row Community Junior School

SAVE THE DOLPHINS

Here is the dolphin. Where has he been?
What has he seen in the deep blue sea?
Dolphin swimming with the sun shining down
With all the other sea creatures all around
Being careful not to get caught
In the fishermen's nets.

Corrina Gunshon (11)
Dean Row Community Junior School

THE RAIN

Drip, drip, drip
The rain, it falls out of the sky.
Drop, drop, drop,
It falls on people passing by.

Drip, drip, drip,
It rains on house and field and wood.
Drop, drop, drop,
The soil it hits, it turns to mud.

Drip, drip, drip,
It can flood us right here, right now.
Drop, drop, drop,
It makes you wonder how.

Drip, drip, drip . . .

Matthew O'Brien (11)
Dean Row Community Junior School

SEA LIFE

Under the sea
Sea life swims gracefully through the calm ocean
Sharks swim slowly ready to snap at their prey
Fish swim quickly away
Dolphins jump in and out the wide ocean happily
Whales squirt water at each other
Octopuses glide through the sea quickly
Jellyfish sit on the bottom of the ocean
Waiting to be carried to shore
Sea life isn't really all that calm.

Claire Blunt (11)
Dean Row Community Junior School

MY LITTLE SISTER PHOEBE

My little sister Phoebe,
She's got blonde and curly hair,
She's normal, bubbly and mischievous,
She's like a cheetah pursuing its prey,
She's a mouse avoiding a cat,
My little sister Phoebe,
Oh how much she makes me laugh.

> My little sister Phoebe,
> Oh how independent she is all the time,
> She's awkward, stubborn and cheeky,
> She's like a lion who's lost its lunch,
> She's a cat trapped in a house,
> My little sister Phoebe,
> Oh how much she makes me laugh.

My little sister Phoebe,
Oh how sleepy she gets sometimes,
She gets shattered, calm, then has bags under her eyes,
She's like a bored lion cub,
She's a rhinoceros, half asleep,
My little sister Phoebe,
Oh how much she makes me laugh.

Joshua James (10)
Dean Row Community Junior School

A POEM ABOUT MY GRANDAD USMAN SAIDE

Under the trees in Africa
Some people were sat
Mending all their tools and clothes
And wearing big straw hats
Never is there enough shade in Africa.

Shade is a rare thing in Africa
As usual in a hot country
I just wish he was here so I could ask him if it was true
Did you ever think life could be so hard
Even though you might not think so.

Jenna Saide (10)
Dean Row Community Junior School

A HOT, SUMMER'S DAY

My favourite day
is a hot summer's day,
where you can
eat ice creams,
go and play!

I go to the swimming baths
or in a paddling pool,
where I relax and
get nice and cool.

Sometimes I get too hot,
and start to get a headache,
but then I go inside
and eat a nice cake.

I go to the shops
to get a nice cold lolly,
then I have a picnic
with my friend Molly.

At the end of the day
I go in my warm bed,
and dream about tomorrow
with my uncle Ted.

Nikita Watkinson (10)
Dean Row Community Junior School

MY FAMILY

Mum says that we all make her glum
Because we act so stupid and dumb.

Dad normally gets really angry and mad,
When I don't clear the table he thinks I've been bad.

Nana has got the most dreadful manner,
I think she acquired it from our neighbour Hannah.

Grandpa Bill is over the hill,
So he has to take a daily pill.

Uncle Guy's got huge big thighs,
A belly to match and bright blue eyes.

Auntie Gertrude is quite rude,
Especially when she eats her food.

Uncle Max (using large, brown sacks),
Has to collect everybody's tax.

Aunt Pam is always in a jam,
But only when she cooks us lamb.

Uncle Fred is a sleepyhead,
He spends all his time curled up in bed.

Aunt Mary works in a colossal dairy,
In her spare time she acts like a fairy.

Uncle Billy is very silly,
All his clothes are pink and frilly.

Auntie Mabel is quite unable
To keep all her horses in their stable.

I am the only sane person in my family,
That's what becomes of having the name Emily.

Katie Waugh (11)
Dean Row Community Junior School

MY NANNY

Nanny, Nanny, no ordinary granny,

My nanny likes to play,
She hates to sit down all day.

She's often seen in the ball pool,
She doesn't care if she looks a fool.

Nanny, Nanny, no ordinary granny,

She knows about Game Boys and PlayStation II,
And all the cheats you have to do,

Pokemon is not a mystery to her mind,

Even when Ekins does his bind,

Nanny, Nanny, no ordinary granny,

She likes to hide her chocolate supply,
And I definitely know why,

We are stuck together like super glue,
That's why I'm never blue,

Nanny, Nanny, no ordinary granny.

Jade Carr (10)
Dean Row Community Junior School

Captain Hook And His Bad Luck

Captain Hook and his inflatable duck
Went strolling into town.
He caught his hook
On a passing truck
And took a bump on his crown.

Jenny Evans (10)
Dean Row Community Junior School

My Darling Dog

My darling dog
He has tan and white fur
Loving, cuddly and cute
Like a woolly mammoth
Like a noisy parrot
It makes me feel loved
Like a mum with a baby
My darling dog
Reminds me of how life can be.

Caitlin Allen (10)
Dean Row Community Junior School

Mathematics

'Pay attention!'
Additions, subtractions,
Working with numbers.
Three dimensions,
Decimals and fractions.
Dividing and multiplying,
'Pay attention!'

Do this sum;
That calculation,
'Now you're in a tricky situation.'
Work it out,
Write it down.
Now you've done an application!

Amy Jo Donoclift (11)
Dean Row Community Junior School

THE SEA

The sea is as blue as the sky
Its horizon is flat, deserted and orange
Usually it is as gentle as a lamb
The gulls swoop down like parachutes coming out of the sky

The waves crashing against the rocks
Its ocean roaring like a lion
The sea's waves rolling like boulders
The sea's undergrowth pounding like a heart

The fish are gleaming like a rainbow
Its whales' reflections shine off the surface
The jellyfish as soft as sheeps fur
The crabs are scuttling like ants

The jet skis whizzing like cheetahs
Men fishing catching their supper
Their oars moving regularly
Swimmers heads bobbing in time with the waves

The sea is dangerous it knows no fear
The sea is destructive like a bomb
It kills like a hawk catching its prey
The sea is forever.

Zac Bagwell (11)
Dean Row Community Junior School

I LOVE MY MUM BUT . . .

I love my mum but . . .
She pinches my chips.
I love my mum but . . .
She nicks my sweets.

I love my mum but . . .
She yells at me.
I love my mum but . . .
She sings in the bath.

I love my mum but . . .
She dances real bad.
I love my mum but . . .
She smokes too much.

I love my mum cos . . .
She does things for me.
I love my mum cos . . .
I know she loves me!

Joshua Jennings (11)
Dean Row Community Junior School

THE GREAT WALL

The Great Wall
Built thousands of years ago
Long, massive, tall
Like a dragon crawling over many hilltops
Like a winding train going through mountains
It makes me so proud
As if a building stuck upon Earth
The Great Wall
Reminds me of the brave people who built it.

Karin Wan (11)
Dean Row Community Junior School

A DAY AT THE TRACTOR-PULLING STADIUM

Loading up my tractor, vroom, vroom, vroom
Off to the stadium, vroom, vroom, vroom
Out we get the tractor, vroom, vroom, vroom
Set up camp, vroom, vroom, vroom

Set the tractor up, vroom, vroom, vroom
On the track we go, vroom, vroom, vroom
Hook the tractor up, vroom, vroom, vroom
Watch the starter for his hand, vroom, vroom, vroom

Off we go, vroom, vroom, vroom
Getting to the end of the track, vroom, vroom, vroom
Get a full pull, vroom, vroom, vroom
Hope you go one day, vroom, vroom, vroom.

Daniel Williams (10)
Dean Row Community Junior School

THE BEACH

The cold blue waves lap over each other onto the beach,
The warm dusty sand blows quickly in clusters,
The slippery seaweed lies calmly on the sea bed,
The boiling bright sunbeams, shine down onto the gleaming water.

The puffy white clouds hang over mountain tops,
The rough multicoloured shells are left behind by the sea,
The scaly fish swim up and down in the cold sea water,
The soft feathery birds glide across the sky slowly.

There are dogs chasing waves, leaving paw prints in the sand,
There are children splashing around in the sea,
There are crabs scuttling across the warm beach,
The clear water sprays the sandy rocks gently.

Hannah Ellwood (11)
Dean Row Community Junior School

ICE CREAM VAN!

'Mum! Can I have one pound,
The ice cream van's here.'
'No! you didn't eat your tea.
'Oh but . . .'
'No!'

Raid the piggy bank,
Got 50p,
I look for some more,
Only one more 50p.

There's 5p in my shoe,
That makes 55p,
Under the bed
There's 20p, that makes 75p now.

What about behind the settee,
There's 20p more,
That makes 95p now,
Just 5p to go.

In the chest of drawers,
There's 10p, that makes . . .
That makes 1 pound,
5p extra, yes!

'Mum! I'm going to
The ice cream van.'
'OK!'
There's the nursery rhyme now,
Oh no, too late, he's gone!

Amy Green (11)
Dean Row Community Junior School

PETS

The rabbits ran round the garden,
Chasing away the cat.
The cat tried to escape,
But he was far too fat.

The cat sat on the mat,
Watching the birds fly by.
Once he caught a bat,
But he'd settle for bird pie.

The bird sat on his perch,
Watching the world go by.
He wished he could be free,
Because he loves to fly.

Thomas Godfrey (10)
Dean Row Community Junior School

BARBADOS

B   arbardos is a Caribbean island
A   paradise island, it is you know, lots of palm trees,
    never snows.
R   oads are so bumpy, uneven not smooth like ours.
B   eautiful sunshine nearly every day.
A   ll the people are so friendly and that makes me smile.
D   ays are so lazy and people go slow, no need to rush,
    lots more days to go
O   h no, it's time to leave, what a super time in Barbados I've had
S   ea, sand and sunshine that's what I had on my visit.

Karl Watkins (10)
Dean Row Community Junior School

THE BIG MATCH

The clock's tick toward 4.30pm.
Slowly and quietly ticks away.
The street's empty.
People shove and push in their hurry
To get to their seats.
Supporters shout for the Reds to win,
Others cheer for the Blues.
People arguing -
It's getting nearer and nearer to full-time
Still 2-2!
Suddenly the Reds score,
Everybody cheers,
Full-time at last!

Ben Rowark (10)
Dean Row Community Junior School

CHIPS

Hot and yummy,
That's how I like them.
Raindrops of vinegar poured on,
Sprinkles of salt, tomato ketchup,
So in under a minute they are all gone!

Out of a paper bag from the chip shop,
On a plate full to the top.
Anywhere they come from,
Any shape or size -
The nicest part of having chips,
Is when they are inside!

Nicky Johnson (11)
Dean Row Community Junior School

THE WEATHER

When the weather is forecast too rain,
People always complain,
The garden needs rain,
But still the people complain!

The weather girl gives out the news,
Tomorrow's going to be bad news,
The morning breaks with gales and gusts,
Mum says, 'Hats and gloves are a must.'

The afternoon starts to blow,
Then the weather starts to snow,
The school bell rings,
It's the end of the day,
Teacher says, 'Off you go out to play.'

Mark Aspinall (10)
Dean Row Community Junior School

THE GIGANTIC WHALE

The gigantic whale
Lives deep in the sea
Black, dark, gloomy
Like the darkness reaching over the sky
Like a hand over the sun
It makes me feel sad
Like a stick just lying there
The gigantic whale
Reminds me of how time goes by.

Jake McKie (10)
Dean Row Community Junior School

ICE CREAM PARADISE

Ice cream,
It's yummy for my tummy,
It's rainy like a boy's nose,
Its different flavours astound you,
Banana, peach, strawberry and mint,
Its cone is like a pyramid,
Its flake is yummy,
But still there is one thing missing,
Of course . . .
It has to be the sauce,
Apple, peach, strawberry and lots more,
And to top it all off, sprinkles on top.

So it's yummy for my tummy!

Parastoo Shayestehroo (10)
Dean Row Community Junior School

MY OLDER SISTER

My older sister
In her teenage years
Athletic, intelligent, a flirt
She's like a star in the sky,
Twinkling, strong and positive.
She makes me feel jealous,
Because she gets all the lads.
My older sister . . .
Let's hope I take after her!

Sophie Tomlinson (11)
Dean Row Community Junior School

THE LITTLE MOUSE

The little mouse
Scurries across the floor
Small, beady-eyed, curious
Like a little spy
Like a fuzzball
It makes me feel like a giant
Like God looking down on Earth
The little mouse
Reminds us how fragile things can be.

Jack Emmons (11)
Dean Row Community Junior School

MY BROTHER

My brother
Is a goody two shoes
He's never asked to clean up
I am

My brother
Plays on the computer
All the time
I do not

My brother
Always makes the mess
But never cleans it up
I do not

My brothers
Never get up in the morning
I have to, so I can clean up
It's not fair!

Stacey Moses (11)
Elworth Hall Primary School

PROPER POORLY

I'm feeling proper poorly
I've caught something off my brother
I've not been to school today
But I'll probably go back tomorrow!

I've had a terribly sore throat
And a dreadful runny nose
I've been in bed all day long
I've even started to speak in prose!

I've read a short book
And watched some telly
I started to do a jigsaw puzzle,
But my bed was like a jelly!

My sore throat's nearly gone
I'm pretty glad about that
But I've still got that awful runny nose
'Atishoo!' Oh drat!

I'm feeling so much better now
It can't have been that bad
I'm looking forward to school
Hang on . . . I must be mad!

Lauren Whalley (10)
Elworth Hall Primary School

THE CHANGE OF THE SEASONS

Spring and Summer are both in the finale
Trying to win for the winning medal.
Summer's in the lead with;
Fireworks
Lazy days
Parties
Laughter
Children
Fun and games.
But Spring's catching up
So he could maybe get in the lead because of;
Happiness
Cucumber
Crocuses
Pussy willow
Bunny rabbits
Kitty cats and lettuce.
Oh great! Summer's taking the lead again,
Come on Summer, win, win, win!
Picnics
Swimming
Sun shining
Full pubs
Birthdays
Sports and holidays.
Spring's getting too hot now,
He's running out of breath
So Summer's taking the lead,
She's getting red now, go on you can do it . . .

Yes!

Jessica Arnold & Rebecca Buttle (10)
Elworth Hall Primary School

I FOUND A DRAGON

I found a dragon,
As small as a rat
Green like summer leaves
Falling from the trees.

With a wizard's book
Brown like tree stumps
Smell like incredible sweet lavender
I can hardly hear it walk.

It sounds a bit like mice
I can hardly believe
A dragon can live in my night-gown,
If I had eaten it,
It would taste like turkey,
That melts in your mouth.

It feels like cobra's skin that just shed itself
I found a dragon as small as a rat,
With a smile
His weird name is Purstard

Just last week
I saw it crying under the car
I gave him a petrol shower
An oil bottle
But the lavender
Did the job.

Luke Legge (10)
Elworth Hall Primary School

SPRING TO SUMMER

Spring is coming to an end
And summer is almost here

BBQs
Picnics
Water fights
Swimming
Holidays
Sun bathing
Ice cream

Summer fights to be free
And now the sun is nice and hot.

Beaches
Daisies
Sunflowers
Ladybirds
Beetles
Birds
Caterpillars

Summer ends in dreadful fear
And now autumn is very near.

Daniel Frost (11)
Elworth Hall Primary School

GRANNY

A granny from London called Nelly
Loved to eat strawberry jelly
She liked it with cream
'Cause it made her beam
When it wobbled around in her belly.

Ashley Madden (11)
Elworth Hall Primary School

THE SKY

When it turns to dusk
And the sky goes pinky-red
I know then that
It is time for bed.

I love the sky
So much,
I wish I was
Big enough to touch
The puffy cotton clouds,
Grey ones,
White ones,
That float all around.

When the sun comes out
And the sky is blue,
It makes me feel so glad,
Blue skies are never sad.

Melissa Lovatt (10)
Elworth Hall Primary School

US RATS

Here I am just watch for me,
Killing humans while they're drinking tea.
I may look cute, I may look nice,
But don't come near me because you'll entice.

Killing humans is my speciality,
Bothering them like a bumblebee.
Going through the forest's mud,
With my feet stamping it like metal studs.

Wooden houses burning down,
Houses like that right down town.
I love their blood, I love their bones,
But I do not like their annoying tones.

I hate sharing with my friends all day,
I've really got to go now so I must say.
I guess you liked to chat with me,
I've got to go now, it's time for tea.

Danny Dunn (10)
Elworth Hall Primary School

DUNKIRK

I was walking through the rows,
Rows of gravestones of the war,
And was reminded of the beach,
The beach of Dunkirk.

The seawater full of blood,
The beach covered with dead bodies,
And the horror of thinking that you're dead already,
And seeing the men die slowly but surely.

The roaring of the engines of the Stukas
And the explosions coming from the bombs.
And Captain John Millar said 'Get on the boats.'
A pleasure boat with room for few.

We escaped the beach of Dunkirk, all six,
It was the worst fortnight of my life.
And I'll never forget it.
The escape of Dunkirk.

Tom J Smith (10)
Kingsley CP School

MY PARENTS

My parents are nice but
they have split up.
I live with my mum on a Sunday
and I live with my dad
every other day.
Sometimes I get upset
but I can live with it.

David Starkey (9)
Kingsley CP School

THE WAR

Bang! Bang! Bang!
Go the bombs being dropped
Bang! Bang! Bang!
Go the guns being shot
Peace on Earth
Is all we want
The war will end soon I hope.

Christopher Dolan (9)
Kingsley CP School

SPRING

The daffodils bring such a good smell,
They don't come in autumn but don't you tell.
I love the sunshine in the spring,
Such a lovely smell the daffodils bring.

Neesha Claire Hunt (9)
Kingsley CP School

HALLOWE'EN

As zombies come out of their bloody graves,
The Devil shouts at his nasty slaves,
They all cry in the middle of the night,
Awakening children with a nasty fright.
As zombies rip people apart,
Vampires' dinner is about to start,
As vampires eat their horrible dinner,
Zombies eat people, thinner and thinner.

Edward Stanley (9)
Kingsley CP School

BATTLE OF BRITAIN

In the days of 1940
The engines buzzed in the sky
The clatter of the guns
The explosions of the bombs
And parachutes all over the sky
Like a white cloud.

Jamie Moores (9)
Kingsley CP School

WOMEN'S WORK

They say that a woman's work is never done.
And I know that this is true,
For even though with all these modern gadgets

The women still have more to do!

Catherine Beck (10)
Kingsley CP School

WISHING WHERE YOU WANT TO BE

We're sitting in the classroom
  Throwing things around
I'm just about to reach some paper
  Then the teacher sends me out!

Walking out the door,
  I murmur to myself,
I wish I was on holiday.
  Flying through the air,
Eating as I want.

Wishing where you want to be,
  Can be so much fun,
I imagine I'm in Benidorm,
  The sun is shining bright,
I'm just about to fall asleep
  And the teacher calls me in,
But wishing where you want to be
  Can still be much more fun.

Chloe Moorcroft (9)
Kingsley CP School

JAILS

Jail's cobwebs on the bars
Spiders crawling on the floor
Exercise mats ripped up
Rowing machines rusty and damp
Beds torn up
Barbed wire sweeping along rusty walls
No one wants to be in a place like this.

Jonathan Skidmore (10)
Kingsley CP School

A WITCH

A witch of death came to school,
And asked who she could kill,
She pointed at me,
I moved left,
She pointed at me again,
I moved right,
She pointed at me again,
I flew up high,
She pointed at me again,
I fell down and cried,
Then I pointed my finger at her,
And she fell down and died.

Jessica McNamara (10)
Kingsley CP School

THE SADNESS OF WAR

Men in war
Men scared
This is the sadness of war.

Men being shot
Men getting wounded
This is the sadness of war.

Men in POW camps
Men being killed in action
This is the sadness of war.

Richard Nimbley (9)
Kingsley CP School

I GET BLAMED FOR EVERYTHING

I get blamed for everything
My mum blamed me for killing the cat
When I didn't, the postman ran over it.

My dad blamed me for eating the cookies
When I didn't, it was my baby brother.

So you see what I mean, I get blamed for everything
My mum blamed me for taking her make-up
But really it was my big sister.

I get blamed for everything and
I got the blame for eating all the chocolate cake.

Wendy Sproston (9)
Kingsley CP School

AT WORK

It's hard being at work
On computers all day
It's hard being at work
Listening carefully to what other people say
It's hard to be a person with too much on your mind
It's hard being at work
All those business sheets to find
It's hard being at work
But there's one thing I know
When you're over 65
You're old and you've got to go!

Sam Kay (9)
Kingsley CP School

SPRING

The daffodils sweetly open their buds.
The roses display their bright colour
And the birds sing their tune
To their lover.

The forest floor looks like a blue carpet
With tall trees in-between,
The squirrels are gathering nuts,
It is a beautiful scene.

The ivy is climbing up a tree,
With fungi at the bottom.
All too soon, when autumn comes again,
The spring will be forgotten.

Rebecca Jane Bell (10)
Kingsley CP School

SWALLOW

If I were a swallow
I would fly
A million miles upon the wing,
Open plains and seas I would spy.

I'd fly then to a warmer land,
When sadly winter came,
And then when summer is here
I'd fly miles back home again.

Hannah Morgan (10)
Kingsley CP School

A WITCH'S DEATH

In 1508
She was led to the stake,
A witch named Elizabeth Wikes.

She is crying out in fury,
Screaming curses at the jury,
Struggling for all she's worth.

She's done nothing wrong,
Just been around for too long,
And now she has to go.

They've got her tied up now,
And she's making an awful row,
Because she doesn't want to die.

The flames are now alight,
And it's the middle of the night,
And she'll never see the light again.

Kate Harrison (10)
Kingsley CP School

MY MUM SAYS . . .

My mum says I'm not allowed to shout,
My dad says I'm not allowed to blow
        bubbles in my chocolate milk,
My sister says to stop smelling,
My brother says to get lost,
My grandma says to keep my hair tidy,
My grandad says to dress tidy,
My uncle says to stop breathing,
I say I'm fine!

Katie Victoria McCausland (10)
Kingsley CP School

A WEEK OF LIMERICKS

There is a day called Monday
Which isn't a very fun-day
Since we're at school it's very uncool,
That horrible day called Monday.

There is a day called Tuesday
That's a nothing-much-to-do day,
Since we're still at school it's very uncool
That horrible day called Tuesday.

There is a day called Wednesday,
Which is a day to cleanse-your-lens day,
Since we're still at school it's very uncool
That horrible day called Wednesday.

There is a day called Thursday,
That's a day to wear-fake-fur day,
Since you have to go to school, it's very uncool,
That horrible day called Thursday.

There is a day called Friday,
Which isn't a day-to-cry day,
Since it's the last day of school, it's very, very cool,
That wonderful day called Friday.

There is a day called Saturday
Which is a doesn't-really-matter day,
Since you're off school, it's very, very cool,
That wonderful day called Saturday.

There is a day called Sunday,
Which leads you on to Monday,
Since tomorrow's school, it's not that cool!
That OK day called Sunday.

Rosie Harrison, Ali Haslam & Emily Taylor (11)
Kingsley CP School

A LIFE OF MYSTERY

I am a fish in the sea,
A rainbow of colours,
Slithering, flittering, through the seas
Glistening blue
One in a million,
One of a crowd,
I live in a world of mystery,
Treasures and charms do I find
As I weave through a colourful coral reef.
But far deep in the murk
Enemies and killers lurk,
There it's a desperate struggle to survive
When and where will my journey end?
And will I ever die?

Victoria Johnson (10)
Little Leigh County Primary School

WOLF

Her howl pierces the murderous night
And blasts the cloud from the sky.
Her fangs glow in the jet-black dark
And her eyes grow cunning and sly.

Animals of the forest
Fear this menacing beast.
Praying they will not be
Her next savage feast.

Ellie Watson (10)
Little Leigh County Primary School

THE MILKY WAY

The Milky Way is so far away,
I can't believe my eyes,
How many planets are up there?
And how big they are in size?
Although they are so far away,
I'd like to visit them one day.
But now I will just have to cope
     by seeing them through my telescope.

Charlotte Leather (10)
Little Leigh County Primary School

MARINE

Waves lap gently upon the sandy shore,
But storms rise up spraying more and
     yet more,
Underwater bubbles and coral and fish,
All the little tails going swish, swish, swish.

Dolphins swim freely, they aren't ever shy,
Gliding up to the surface, facing the sky,
Coral and seaweed float slowly around,
And if you look closely, even more can
     be found.

Swimming in the sea can be just like a ride,
It's amazing just how much the ocean
     can hide.

Rachel Gover (11)
Mossley CE Primary School

BOOKS

Witches and wizards, magic and spell books,
Castles and horses, fierce pirates with hooks.
Smugglers, ships, treasure, seamen galore,
Take a look at a few; you'll be pleading for more!

Mythical creatures, there's a phoenix, a dragon!
Farmers, fields, country pubs, mead in a flagon.
The past, the present, the future, whatever!
Anything goes, just never say never!

Never-ending chocolate supplies, plenty of sweets,
I'm an Olympic runner, going for gold in the heats.
Fluttering fairies, flying children, Peter Pan,
Up in space, flying high, on the moon the first man.

Deep-sea submarines, searching wrecks sunk in times gone by,
Spiralling down aeroplane, no longer way up high.
Monsters, ghosts, skeletons, ghouls, all in a haunted house,
Watch out if you set traps - on a mission there's a mouse.

Adventures, horror, fantasy - I'm stuck in a cave!
I'm a goalie in Man United - oh what a save!
Share ideas, swap 'em, make one up with your mates,
Just let your mind go - aren't stories great?

Laura Thomas (11)
Mossley CE Primary School

PAINT

I love to paint,
though I'm not a saint.
I use all Mum's money,
and she goes all funny.

I love to paint,
though I'm not a saint.
I paint the sun,
and it's loads of fun.

I love to paint,
though I'm not a saint.

Sarah Poyser & Lydia Butter (11)
Mossley CE Primary School

SENSE POEM - THE IRON WOMAN

I see dark, black, poisonous, muddy
water flowing along the marsh.

I smell polluted fumes and rotting
marsh creatures.

I hear *screaming* marsh creatures
dying in the marsh.

I taste polluted, toxic, murky,
black water

I feel *livid* and I want to destroy the
ignorant ones.

Michael Parry (9)
Murdishaw West CP School

PYRAMIDS

Pyramids black as night
Bright yellow paintings in the tomb
Gods dancing on the walls
Pictures of shimmering gold
Mountains of silver shining like stars
Rows of rubies next to the king
Pearls white as snow
Dazzling in the dark.

Ryan Stevenson (10)
Murdishaw West CP School

WHAT I KNOW IS THAT

A black cat is like a shadow climbing a tree
A star is like streetlights
A chair is like a stone carving
A television is like a cardboard box
A car is like a blackboard
A clock is like a plate with two knives
A crying baby is like bells
A book is like a present you can open
again and again.

Michael Clucas (10)
Murdishaw West CP School

MY HOUSE

Marmalade-peel bricks built from the ground
Sloping golden roof reaching the sky
Shiny tiles like sandcastles on the beach
Chimney like a box of chocolates
Puffs out peppermint creams.

Eyes winking in the dark
Curtains closed at night keep out cold
Gingerbread door opens wide
Jellybean chair holds the family
Carpets of velvet under my feet
My dream house came true.

Joanne Forshaw (11)
Murdishaw West CP School

SENSE POEM - IRON WOMAN

I see factory-polluted waste splashing
out into clean water.
I smell polluted factory fumes.
I hear the shout for help in the marsh
of the creatures.
I feel angry at the ignorant ones at the
poisonous factory.
I tasted the polluted water coming out
of my mouth.

Nathan Pugh (10)
Murdishaw West CP School

SCARY PYRAMIDS

Pointed pyramids dark and gloomy
Mummies inside do not look happy
Slaves outside building brick by brick
Inside the tomb most scary
Scarab beetles scurry beneath you
Mountains of gold in the monstrous tomb
Gods on the walls guarding the glittering gold.

Adam Kneale (9)
Murdishaw West CP School

SENSE POEM - IRON WOMAN

I see the marsh creatures dying because
of the dangerous factory waste.
I smell the factory flooding the marsh
with all its waste.
I hear the crying of the sick creatures.
I taste the poisonous water running through me.
I feel that the factory is polluting the marsh
                              on purpose.

Aimee Jade Foran (9)
Murdishaw West CP School

WHAT I KNOW IS THAT

A star is like a wish with a flashlight
A black cat is like a shadow following you in the dark
A book is like a land where no one can find you
A crying baby is like wedding bells
A car is like a blackboard
A television is like a house
A chair is like a stone carving
A clock is like a plate with two knives.

Samantha Manley (10)
Murdishaw West CP School

CATHERINE WHEEL

Rainbow colours bursting out
Sparks fluttering into the darkness
Spinning wheel swirling and fizzing
The screeching and screaming annoys me.

Catherine wheels spurting out fancy rubies
Yellow balls like the golden sun
Sparks spitting out like the juice of an orange
Sapphires flashing like stars in the night
The brilliant stars amaze me.

Ryan McKibbin (11)
Murdishaw West CP School

SENSE - IRON WOMEN

I see the disgusting black waste from
                                    that terrible factory.
I smell the poisoned creatures I loved the most.
I hear the wailing groan from the dying poisoned creatures.
I taste the slimy, grass snakes slithering in the marsh.
I feel livid about those ignorant mean murderers.

Kimberley Greene (10)
Murdishaw West CP School

WHAT I KNOW IS THAT

A black cat is like a shadow in the sunlight
A star is like a ball of fire
A chair is like a stone carving
A car is like a rocket blasting off
A television is like a doll's house
A clock is like a plate with a knife and fork
A crying baby is like a motorbike
A book is like a present you can open
again and again.

Ryan Killen (10)
Murdishaw West CP School

SENSE POEM - IRON WOMAN

I see weeds and dead creatures.
I smell disgusting dirty waste from the factory.

I hear the splashing of the marsh eels.
I taste mouth-watering poisonous water.
I feel livid about the nasty ones at the
                              dangerous factory.

Jade Mills (9)
Murdishaw West CP School

SENSE POEM - IRON WOMAN

I see dying creatures.
I smell horrid, murky, polluted waters.
I hear the *scream* of the dying creatures.
I taste the mud and roots pouring out of my mouth.
I feel *livid,* hurt and angry to watch the
dying creatures as I come from the marsh.

Loren Ashton (9)
Murdishaw West CP School

TUTANKHAMUN

The Boy King ruled Egypt
Wearing collars of dazzling gold
On his head a slithering snake
A crook and flail on his hand
Silver sandals on his feet
Living happily in the afterlife.

Danny Roscoe (9)
Murdishaw West CP School

THE MAGICAL NILE

Inky waters and dancing waves
The floating, flowing life of Egypt
Bobbing boats sailing home
Banks flood year after year
New green growth on the banks
Men downstream get reeds and fish
Reeds of papyrus telling their story
Hippo hunts day after day
Reflecting the charm and enchantment
Of the magical, mystical Nile.

Justin Lewis (9)
Murdishaw West CP School

SENSE POEM - IRON WOMAN

I see the dead sea creatures lying on the
soaking muddy water
I smell the salty polluted marsh
I hear the weeds drooping into the watery
mud splishing and sploshing
I taste the pollution gargling in my gigantic
                                      metal mouth
I feel furious with the people who caused the
damage to the water and the creatures!

Mesha McManaman (9)
Murdishaw West CP School

EGYPTIAN TREASURES

Statue cats, sparkling silver
Scarlet rubies beaming red
Ivory tusks, milky pearls piled like snow
Shimmering, glimmering collars
Amulets as gold as the sun
Gleaming, glittering see-through diamonds
As bright as the stars
Chariots of precious jewels
Carrying the Pharaoh to life after death
Spears and axes as sharp as a blade
Defend the king in the tomb.

John Porter (9)
Murdishaw West CP School

SENSE POEM - IRON WOMAN

I see the mist of the horrid waste.
I smell the poisonous polluted fumes circling
all around me.
I hear the horrid dreadful sounds of the
crying wails for help, joining them are the
injured animals of the marsh.
I taste the foul-polluted ground flooding with
waste and pollution.

Kelsey Howarth (9)
Murdishaw West CP School

SENSE POEM - IRON WOMAN

I see the dirty factory turning the lovely
clean water into horrible disgusting water
I smell the poisonous fumes coming from
                              the tall factory
I hear the cry of all the hurting animals of
                              the marsh
I taste the deadly polluted water flooding
                              out of my mouth
I feel livid about the stupid workers of
                              the factory.

Claire Quinn (9)
Murdishaw West CP School

SENSE POEM - IRON WOMAN

I see the predictable chemical waste
pumping into the water.

I see the reeds tormenting my spinal cord.

I hear the gasping cries for help from
                              the marsh creatures.

I taste runny soil squirming around my mouth.

I feel the perspiration streaming down my
                              neck in anger.

John Cuddy (10)
Murdishaw West CP School

WHAT I KNOW IS THAT

A chair is like a stone carving
A car is like a blackboard
A crying baby is like wedding bells
A television is like a doll's house
A black cat is like a black phantom spirit
A book is like a present you can open
                                again and again
A star is like Cupid's arrow
A clock is like a bowl which never gets washed.

Leon Randles (9)
Murdishaw West CP School

TREASURES

Treasure so shiny, bright and glittery
Golden yellow like the sun
Rubies, red like a rose
Red as the colour of blood
Pearls, white and shining
White like snow so cold
Golden necklaces for around the neck
Shining headdress on the head
Mountains of silver-like stars at night
All this treasure in the tomb.

Amanda Orme (9)
Murdishaw West CP School

SENSE POEM - IRON WOMAN

I see the dirty, black and muddy water.
I smell toxic waste which is polluting the water.
I hear the *scream* of the dying creatures
from the marsh.
I taste the poisonous squirting out my mouth.
I feel livid about the dying creatures
from the factory waste.

Jenna Brown (9)
Murdishaw West CP School

THE HEADLESS HORSEMAN

On October 31st every year,
The horseman comes out to hunt.
He holds his sword and waits,
To have his little fun.

Suddenly he hears a noise,
Of three men coming his way.
He hides in the bushes,
Then jumps out at his prey.

The men are startled,
And frozen stiff with fear.
The horseman rides at them
And now the horseman's near.

Swish! Swash! The sword goes wild,
The horseman looks for a head.
The headless man falls to the ground
And the horseman returns to his bed.

Guy Watmore (10)
Pownall Hall School

THERE WAS AN OLD MAN FROM PENZANCE

There was an old man from Penzance,
Who had about fifty great aunts.
When one of them died,
He cried and he cried
And wet his bright yellow frayed pants.

Matthew Thistleton (10)
Pownall Hall School

THE SNAKE

Slithering silent through the jungle fern
With glittering eyes that looked at me as
I pulled up my net.
There surfed a cobra across the jungle floor
And this I saw him do.
He pulled up his neck and rattled his vicious jaws.
A mongoose scampered, and bit him on the tail.
I lifted up my net and caught them with delight.

Dominic Dykstra (11)
Pownall Hall School

THE FROG

My frog named Stump
Is a green, fat lump.
He sits on the grass
That great spotted mass
And watches me
With small beady eyes
Thinking about a plate of flies.

Cameron Bell (10)
Pownall Hall School

MY FAVOURITE TEACHER

I have a favourite teacher,
Mrs Hindley is her name.
Setting difficult English tests,
Is her little game.

She likes to tell jokes,
But then she sets a test.
She also likes the hunky blokes,
But that's not all the rest.

If you're really, really good,
She will not give you the vice.
But if you are really bad,
Let's say it is not nice.

James Kendall (11)
Pownall Hall School

AREA 52

The secret place,
Where the armies trained,
Always sought but never found,
The trainees love the hidden place,
But never tell and never will.

The secret place,
Where experiments begin,
Discoveries made but never told,
Complex chemicals found around,
Where is it?
Nobody knows.

Alexander Staniland (10)
Pownall Hall School

RACHAEL'S RAINBOW

Creamy-coloured clouds held my rainbow
thoughts high up in the eternal blue . . .

Rooster's call awakes me from my heavenly dreams
Oval moon half-sunken in the autumn orange horizon
Yolk in my egg to top up my tummy until lunch
Grass is showered in dew-like speckles of glue
I felt happy inside and a warm feeling
Vowed never to forget the morning . . .

Rainbow

Rachael Heaviside (10)
Pownall Hall School

THE RAG DOLL

The rag doll lies
Its mouth open in silent cries
Its stark white face
Its miniature clothes of lace
Its face littered with flies.

Its eyes gaze at the sun
Burning its face shaped as a bun
It will always remain in that ditch
Always ready to snitch
The story of the rag doll.

Alexander Lawrence (10)
Pownall Hall School

THE EXAM

I sit in the car, waiting for the gates to open.
Today is the day of my exam.
I feel nervous, I feel tired, I feel frustrated.
My mother says,
that with all the work I've been doing,
I should feel prepared.
Just the opposite.
All I can think of is a man standing there
making sure I don't talk.
And another man, there to see who he can
throw away on the first paper.
Someone knocks on my car window,
'Time to go,' he says.
I step out of my car and follow him to
the Classroom of Death.

Patrick Mullarkey (11)
Pownall Hall School

MONSTER FROM THE NIGHT

The monster from the night
It might give you a fright
It hangs upside down
Turning round and round
Calling 'Kill! Kill! Kill!
I will eat what I
Will! Will! Will!'

'Are you scared?'
You say, you say.
'Why should I be scared?
It's the middle of the day!'

Heather Crawford (11)
Rainow Primary School

KENNINGS DOG

Slipper-chewer
Flea-scratcher
Food-guzzler
Foot-snuzzler
Kennel-sleeper
Lap-sitter
Cat-chaser
Fast-walker
Loud-barker
Fur-loser
Fire-warmer
Soft-biter
Treat-eater
Bone-burier
Water-drinker
Wet-licker

Alison Werrell (9)
Rainow Primary School

THE WHIZ KID.COM

He stared at his computer screen
It made me feel *I want to scream!*
His brain *had gone . . !*
Whilst he was visiting Kids.Com.
He gawped and gawped with no real thought . . .
He doesn't know a thing he's taught.
So he just loaded another game.
No one knows if he's quite sane.

Benjamin D Evans (10)
Rainow Primary School

KENNINGS SNAKE

Body-binder
Mouse-gorger
Jaw-dislocator
Scaly-slitherer
Skin-shedder
Cold-blooded
Rock-rubber
Forked-tongue
Elongated-cylinder
Heat-lover
Night-roamer
Scream-maker
Paralysing-poisoner
Hypnotic-starer
Death-squeezer
Curly-twister
Side-winder
Multi-coloured
Shape-changer
Soft-invertebrate
Snake-handbag.

Thomas Richmond (10)
Rainow Primary School

WHIZZING CAR

A car is like a zooming rocket
Speeding down the highway.
The enormous engine roars
Into action as the windows wind down,
Then the cool air floods in.
But a car can be like a gas bomb polluting the air as it comes.

Michael Waters (10)
Rainow Primary School

THERE WAS A YOUNG PIG FROM DOVER

There was a young pig from Dover,
Who had a brand new Rover,
He had a terrible itch,
And drove into a ditch
That silly young pig from Dover.

Victoria Briggs (9)
Rainow Primary School

MY BROTHER

My brother's called Ben,
He can now count up to ten,
He eats hot chicken,
Gets ketchup over his lips,
Some nights he stays up till ten.

Edward Manders-Naden (11)
Rainow Primary School

SONNET

If I were to write a sonnet,
I'd start with a blank sheet in my mind,
Then I'd think what to put on it,
Leaving all my worries behind.

I'd choose the pen and the colour of ink,
I'd find the paper that matches,
Without restraint I'd let myself think,
And a brand new poem hatches.

The words would dance from my pen,
My thoughts would play the tune,
I'd lose all sense of where and when,
Till the sun gives way to the moon.

My pen would go down, lid on ink,
And into my bed I'd softly sink.

Caitlin Doherty (10)
Rainow Primary School

THERE WAS A . . .

There was a young dad of Dumbree
Who never drank his tea
For he ate his cake
And put on such weight
That silly young dad from Dumbree!

Jodie Leicester (11)
Rainow Primary School

THE LION

The lion sees his prey and licks his lips at the sight.
His lissom, lithe body leaps over the ground.
His long, lean legs stretch out and he catches his prey.
Lazily he lies down, spreading out after the lovely meal.

Holly Bailey (8)
Rushton CE Primary School

THE FIRE

Fire, the spirit of destruction, can eat up all
                              the land
Fierce heat, flames and a roaring voice is fire.
Red, yellow, orange, glittering colours glow
                             against the sky.

Hot, golden light fills up this magical night,
But at dawn it has gone and left just ashes
                            and dust.

Georgia Plimbley (8)
Rushton CE Primary School

ICE

Crystal snowflakes fall.
Ground's cold.
Winter's call.
White clouds.
Snow is glistening
Snow starts to mould.
Freezing solid.
Children play in glistening snow.

Frosted ears running nose.
This weather is as light as a feather.
Frozen pond.
Children are fond
Of whistling snow.
The snails are not out.
I'm glad because they are slow.
No sand.
Iced land.

Emma Edwards (9)
St Augustine's RC Primary School, Runcorn

SCABBY, THE EVIL CREATURE

This monster is . . .

Scarier than a killer shark gnashing his teeth.

Uglier than you with chickenpox.

Higher than a bird flapping its wings in the sky.

Faster than the fastest animal you can imagine.

Spikier than a pair of antler's horns.

Greedier than one person eating a hundred pies.

Slimier than a witch's skin falling off her.

More wrinkly than a miserable granny shouting at children.

Kate Hunter (9)
St Basil's Primary School, Widnes

THE X-CLOPS

This monster is . . .

Scarier than a great white shark jumping up at you.

Fatter than Henry VIII when he was forty-three.

Speedier than a cheetah running after a deer.

More fearsome than a lion hunting its prey.

Heavier than an African elephant eating fifty buns.

More wrinkly than an old granny rocking in a chair.

Uglier than a fat, hairy tarantula crawling out of a log.

Rachel Delahunty (9)
St Basil's Primary School, Widnes

THE SUBJECT OF THIS POEM IS . . .

The subject of this poem is . . .
As tall as twenty trees on top of each other
As clever as a cheetah
As greedy as a pig

As heavy as a Sumo wrestler
As scary as a ghost
As naughty as a robber
As uncaring as a lion

As bouncy as a bouncy ball
As playful as a kitten
As hard as nails
As thick as two short planks of wood

As ugly as a vampire
As busy as a bee
As loud as a radio on full blast
As selfish as a spider.

James McInerney (8)
St Basil's Primary School, Widnes

THE ZINCH

This monster is
Scarier than a one-eyed Cyclops in the bath
Faster than a cheetah with rocket boosters
Heavier than ten hippos put together.

Fatter than an elephant that's just eaten his dinner
Slimier than a snail slithering along
Scalier than a snake with lots of scales
Hairier than a baboon banging on his head.

David Hyland (9)
St Basil's Primary School, Widnes

THE SUBJECT OF THIS POEM IS . . .
(For my grandad Dougie, who died on January 15th 2001)

The subject of this poem is . . .

As intelligent as Einstein,
As brave as a lion,
As happy as can be,
As reliable as man's best friend.

As loving as a hug from Mum,
As friendly as a newborn puppy,
As cuddly as a cushion,
As safe as parents' love.

As impatient as a toddler,
As busy as a bee,
As special as God's universe,
That's what you mean to me.

Alexander J Hill (9)
St Basil's Primary School, Widnes

THINKINGSTELLA

This monster is . . .
Slower than a mountain with no legs
Greener than the darkest green
More intelligent than a teacher with a potion
More loveable than a marriage taken place in a church
Thinner than a skinny twig that's been chopped in half
Smellier than sixty dustbins in a big hall
Brainier than one hundred teachers putting their brains together
Stronger than six million men put together lifting a big giant
Clumsier than a person who's just learnt how to drive.

Chloé Holland (9)
St Basil's Primary School, Widnes

HALF ASLEEP

Half asleep
And half awake
You don't know what you are about to do because
You are alone, alone on your own.

When aeroplanes go roaring by
As they fly, fly, fly
I go to sleep and hear a beep
From a car nearby.

The rustling of some pages in a favourite story book,
The murmuring and mutters and
The clattering while Mum cooks.

The splashing of the rain
I hear on my windowpane
The miaowing of the cat
As he scratches on the kitchen mat.

Lucy-May Amos Roscoe (9)
St Basil's Primary School, Widnes

HORMONK

Hormonk
Is a cheater in games like me.
Is cleverer than a cafe full of people.
Is slower than a slithery worm.
Is smarter than my mum going to the fords.
Is faster than a wiggly worm going to town.
Is taller than a giraffe standing on its two back legs.
Is nicer than a flower, just been picked.
Is angrier than a monkey with no bananas left.

Ashley Horrocks (8)
St Basil's Primary School, Widnes

THE SUBJECT OF THIS POEM IS . . .

As tough as leather
As good as gold
As smooth as silk
As green as mould

As intelligent as the most advanced computer
As frightening as a ghost
As quick as lightning
As deaf as a post

As dreaded as a tooth been pulled out
As graceful as a swan
As long as the Nile
As playful as Pokémon

What is it?

Tom Fry (9)
St Basil's Primary School, Widnes

JAMIE'S BEDROOM

In my bedroom I kept

Ten slim dogs chewing the bed,
Nine chickens laying eggs in my slippers,
Eight cats trying to get in the goldfish bowl,
Seven scared goldfish trying to get out of the bowl,
Six hairy, fat pigs making sausages in the wardrobe,
Five white mice hanging from the television,
Four rolling sheep chewing the carpet,
Three fierce donkeys charging at the door,
Two confused horses banging into the wall and
One big mess 'Drat'!

Jamie Findlater (8)
St Basil's Primary School, Widnes

HAYLEY AND LISA'S RAP

Hey, I am Lisa
And this is Hayley
We are not best friends
But we could be

We both get homework
We both go to school
We go to the best
One called St Basil's
It rules!

We had two teachers
Called Blunty and Ken
And as you can see
They're both horrible men

They moan and groan
At us all the time
They are always drunk
But only on wine

We both like dancing
As you can see
We both like football
So we're good company

We both like music
We both hate boys
Especially Sam
He makes too much noise

But unfortunately
We can't rap no more
And as we can see
You're all running for the door

But please don't go
Stick around till ten
And if you liked us
Come and see us again.

Hayley McCann & Lisa Thomas (10)
St Basil's Primary School, Widnes

MY HEADMASTER

I like my headmaster
He is very kind
He sometimes can be thoughtful
And he has a great mind.

Some different headmasters
Are very, very grumpy
But I start laughing at some
That are very crumpy.

I don't like headmasters
That have the mumps
And some headmasters are
Thick as tree trunks.

Some posh headmasters
Have very big houses
But most of them are
Scared of mouses.

Some silly headmasters
Think they are in the groove
But they are not because
They show off at the moves.

Andrew McDonagh (9)
St Basil's Primary School, Widnes

HALLOWE'EN NIGHT

Hallowe'en is the best
Lots of nasty witches
And all the rest
Spooky creepy ditches
Where cats and bats stray

Now it's time for the witches to come out
With their spooky broomsticks
I love to go about
I like to do some black magic tricks.

I like to go around the streets
With my creepy croaking voice
I get lots of treats
From the houses in my streets.

That's Hallowe'en.

Rachael Horrocks (10)
St Basil's Primary School, Widnes

HALLOWE'EN

It was a black spooky night,
The mood was just right,
For witches to mix their spells,
The cauldron was bubbling,
The witches were cackling,
While chanting their nasty spells.

Hopping around upon the ground,
Slimy toad everywhere
And the black witch's cat
On her broomstick she sat,
While purring her contented purr.

Twinkling in the moonlight
Big black bats are the only sight,
Flying up ever so high,
Lots of them passing by,
Big black bats rule the sky.

Brogan Gillbanks-Morgan (9)
St Basil's Primary School, Widnes

FRIENDS

Yo, this is a rap
By Helen and Rebecca
One is small and one is tall
People say we are good together
Best friends forever and ever.

Whatever we do,
Whatever we say
We work as a team
Night and day.

When it is school
We begin our lesson
'Cause we were so naughty
We keep on messin'

After school we head for tea
It's normally veg and broccoli,

When it's bedtime,
We snuggle up tight
We ring each other up
To say goodnight.

Helen Crowder & Rebecca Foran (10)
St Basil's Primary School, Widnes

NIGHT NOISES

When I go up to bed
I am half asleep and half awake

I hear
People shouting
Babies kicking
Lights going off and on
Creaking floorboards
Dogs barking
Mums chatting
Wind blowing
Mugs crashing
Children clapping
Birds singing
Nans laughing
TV talking
Doors slamming
Fish swimming
Then I hear nothing - nothing at all
Because I'm asleep, sound asleep.

Jeniffer Turner (8)
St Basil's Primary School, Widnes

A POEM FOR SPECIAL PEOPLE

When you have had a bit of a bash,
The paramedics will be there in a flash.
The fire services go very fast,
When you have a fire they give it a blast.

Even if the gas station is mad,
If petrol burns it can hurt very bad,
If there is a person in a flush,
The services will be more of a rush.

The doctors help you if you're sick,
They will give you medication quick.
The police will catch dreaded people,
Sometimes the criminal may be feeble.
If there is a crash in the busy street,
The police will come in a very big fleet.

Emily Davidson (10)
St Basil's Primary School, Widnes

TODAY AT SCHOOL

First we're doing history,
After that geography,
We're going to get real smart,
Then we're doing art.

Also we're doing a display,
I'm going to put it in my tray.
I'm going to use my pencil case,
And then I'll fasten my shoe lace.

We are making our own creature,
I really do *not* like my teacher.
Then we're going to the baths,
After that it's maths.

I think our class is cool,
But I don't like my school.
The funniest thing is my slippers,
For lunch I had cream dippers.

Our best teacher, is the PE coach,
Once in the cupboard, I found a cockroach,
Our teacher is really fun,
But lifting weights, weighs a ton.

Sean Willis (10) & Robert Johnson
St Basil's Primary School, Widnes

OUR CLASS

This is a rap about our crazy funky class!

When Hannah walks she steps a mile,
When Louis writes it takes a while.
When Kelly sings, she does it a lot,
When Vicky's in maths she always says *wot.*

Tom is always *late,*
Mr Blunt hates to wait.
Kerri likes to run
Everyone in the class likes to have some *fun!*

Martyn likes to fight
Adam likes to play out all night
Sam always sucks his thumbs

These are all Hannah's, Vicky's and Kerri's best chums!

Kerri Unsworth, Hannah Corrigan (9) & Victoria Cody (10)
St Basil's Primary School, Widnes

A NEW BEGINNING

Playing for a fresh football team and playing all the games,
Feeling very timid because you don't know any names.
Hitting the ball about on the floor,
Hoping the manager won't show you the door.

Going training every Thursday night,
Hoping you won't get in a fight.
Getting used to the manager and not knowing his name,
Hoping you turn out like Owen and have a lot of fame.

Now I have started to know their names,
I am also playing in a lot more games.
I have started laughing and joking with them more,
But once I nearly broke my toe.

Sean Wright (11)
St Basil's Primary School, Widnes

SCHOOL STARTS

A new beginning,
A fresh start,
A school uniform makes me look smart.

New books and new pens,
The school terms never end,
New classrooms settling in,
Strict teachers make you flinch.

Lots of homework on Friday night,
It is exactly one metre in height.

A new person in our class,
I wonder if this girl will last?
A girl before was name called,
I wonder if this girl will stand strong?

Every things fine, it's the end of the day,
It's time to go home and have a play.

I'm looking forward to tomorrow,
I will have lots of fun and there will be no sorrow.

There's only one problem left in this term
I don't want to leave at the end of the year.

Lauren Berry (10)
St Basil's Primary School, Widnes

PLATERCER

The platercer is . . .
Bigger than the Jolly Green Giant on stilts,

He is thinner than a pencil being squashed,

He is faster than the speed of light with a jet pack on,

He is cleverer than Einstein with four million brains,

He is quieter than a pin being dropped five thousand miles away,

He is stronger than a giant exercising with houses,

He is hairier than a spider growing a beard,

He is richer than the richest king in the world
Who won one million pounds in poker.

Daniel Wright (9)
St Basil's Primary School, Widnes

MY ALIEN FRIEND

My alien friend has a green nose,
He has six fingers and six toes.
He has three eyes at the top of his head,
And he wears his spacesuit when he goes to bed.

He has toast in his cereal for breakfast, and a cup of tea,
He painted a picture for me of a purple tree,
One day he came to school with me and said hello to my teachers,
He scared her out of the classroom and since then I've never seen her.

Just a few days ago he went back into space,
He went back to the planet Zog and for a while, I've never seen
                                        his face.

Laura Griffiths (10)
St Basil's Primary School, Widnes

SCHOOL ROCKS

I like school,
It's really cool.
My teacher can shout,
She will blow you out.

The bully thinks the school is a drool
But I just think he's a stupid fool.
When you're having your dinner and he hears you munch,
I will come right over and give you a punch.

My favourite subject is art
Because it really blows me apart.
All of my friends think school knocks
But I just think it really rocks.

I've got a really clever friend
But he just drives me round the bend.

Tom Floyd & Glen Shone (9)
St Basil's Primary School, Widnes

THE OBJECT OF THIS POEM

As boring as watching paint dry
As long as a snake
As difficult as finding your way out of a maze
As tricky as a flea
As tiring as climbing a mountain
As rewarding as winning a marathon
As noisy as a football crowd
As challenging as an eternity puzzle.

Sarah Farrelly (9)
St Basil's Primary School, Widnes

OUR SCHOOL

We both go to school
And it's really cool
Wednesday and Friday
We go to the baths
And all week long
We learn some maths
I'm the one who's really cool
And my friend is the one who is a fool

Some people think that they're the best
But I'm the one who's better than the rest
Nancy always bites her nails
And Craig always tells the tales

I'm good at art
And she's very smart
Most of the time we spend in class
Sometimes we go to mass
Some people say this is the school of hard knocks
But we think our school really rocks.

Louis Donovan (9) & Ben Mahon (10)
St Basil's Primary School, Widnes

BONFIRE NIGHT

Dark still November night,
Colours explode, bursting bright,
Crackle, snackle, whizz, pop,
Rockets zooming, to Earth they drop.

Exploding really bright
Rockets bang and give you a fright,
Snackle, crackle, whoosh, bang,
Catherine wheels go twang.

Fireworks, fireworks in the sky,
People being silly with them, I don't know why,
Crash, wallop, boom, splosh,
Treacle toffee in mouths go squash!

All night long *boom, boom, boom,*
People amazed at the Roman tomb,
Crash, fizzle, twizzle, swoosh,
Bonfire Night is really grand.

Paul Brookfield (11)
St Basil's Primary School, Widnes

A NEW BEGINNING IN YEAR SIX

A new fresh start in year six,
So many more worries,
So many more hopes,
Lots of homework to do every night.

So many books,
Lots of work to do.
No one gets away with not doing their homework right.
New classroom.

New teacher,
Jobs to do every playtime,
Take care of the young children.
Every morning I wake up
I don't want to go to school,
It's noisy like a stampede,
Hard work to do,
Silence all the time,
I always beg to just go home.

Jennifer O'Neill (11)
St Basil's Primary School, Widnes

THE SUBJECT OF THIS POEM IS . . .

As curly as a spring
As ugly as a bulldog's face,
As fat as an elephant,
As fast as a cheetah in a race.

As smelly as a skunk,
Teeth as sharp as a rhino's horn,
As dirty as a pig's dinner,
As white as a daisy.

As playful as a kitten,
As nosy as a neighbour
As soft as a mitten.

What is it?

Paul Smith (9)
St Basil's Primary School, Widnes

I WAS A PLUM

I was a small plum
Hanging from a tree
As happy as can be.

Singing with my family while eating my tea
I was ripped from my home.

I felt scared.
I rolled over the other plums.
I got taken to this huge place.

The next day a huge hand picked me up
And took me to someone's home.
Then I knew I was going to be someone's tea!

Matthew McDonough (9)
St Basil's Primary School, Widnes

A New School Year

A fantastic new school year,
Special, fun and fresh,
Lots and lots of new things here,
The days packed full, no time to mess.

A new teacher called Miss Ryan,
The boss of the school,
She'll make us all start crying,
If we even try to play the fool.

Hard work and new books,
Clean, tidy, amused,
Miss Ryan thinking she has good looks,
Keeps us all amused.

Two days of fun,
Then work, work, work,
PE, it's rounders, I've got to run,
High school kids look on and smirk.

I was really excited
Before I started school,
But now I'm really, really tired
Of all Miss Ryan's rules.

I really think I'm settling in,
With my new desk and place to sit,
After Christmas I'll learn to swim,
Hope this year is a hit.

Emily Allen (10)
St Basil's Primary School, Widnes

School Is Cool

We all go to St Basil's school,
It is wicked, it is cool.
In our school there's loads of creatures,
The worst of them all is just our teachers.
When it's time to eat our dinner,
We aren't getting any thinner.
After dinner we're doing a display,
Mrs McCabe said 'Put 'em on your tray.'
Soon we're doing a groovy mass,
We're gonna split it between each class.
Next we're gonna be doing art,
We don't dress up very smart.
When we're wearing funky slippers,
Mrs McCabe wears big blue flippers.
Now it's time to say goodbye,
Goodbye!

Paige Reed & Victoria Mottram (10)
St Basil's Primary School, Widnes

My Grandad!

My grandad is old
But hardly bold
He has a smile
Just once in a while

He is a bit grumpy
His belly is rather bumpy
Sometimes he is happy
Sometimes he is sad
Don't be naughty you will make him so mad.

He can be very funny
And he can be very tight with his money
He has got tatty hair
But he does not care
That is my grandad,
The best in the world.

Jodie Harrison (9)
St Basil's Primary School, Widnes

MY MIND IS IN SPACE

My mind is in space,
It takes off like a rocket,
It circles all the planets
But never comes back to Earth.

It goes to Saturn,
It goes to Mars,
It doesn't take long
Because there's no cars.

My mind is in space,
It seems like it caused the big bang,
Otherwise . . .
I would not think.

It goes to Uranus,
It goes back to Mars,
It goes to Mercury,
All I have to do is dodge the stars.

My mind is in space,
It zooms round and round,
I came to the Milky Way
And thought I had to stop.

Craig Rose (10)
St Basil's Primary School, Widnes

THE SUBJECT OF THIS POEM IS . . .

As friendly as can be,
As good as gold,
As hard as a brick.

As healthy as me,
As cool as a pop star,
As loud as a giant,
As powerful as a bull.

As tricky as a maze,
As quick as a cheetah,
As sharp as a knife,
As spooky as a ghost.

As cheeky as a chimp,
As smooth as a book,
As hot as the sun,
As greedy as a pig.

Who is it?

Chris McGowan (8)
St Basil's Primary School, Widnes

MY BABY SISTER

When I first saw my sister
She looked a real trickster.
My mum said leave her alone,
Went down the corridor, sat on my own.

At eleven o'clock I went home,
The next day we went to Blackpool.
When we came back
I jumped straight on my bed.

When my sister became a lot older
She got a pain in the neck.
I felt like smacking her the whole time
But I couldn't because I would've got a crack.

All the family was happy,
Even my little sister Abbie.
The next door neighbour was buying presents,
We all celebrated in my house.

Carl Pye (10)
St Basil's Primary School, Widnes

NEW BEGINNINGS

I remember starting school,
Very worrying if I lose the games.
Having a teacher
I do not know,
Meeting other people,
Oh no.
Very scared of my teacher
In the winter.

People have been nasty to me,
Making me cry,
I want to go home,
Don't want to stay,
I don't know where to go.
Food to be free,
No more work,
No more bossing me about,
Mum please don't shout!

But I love to be the top of the school
Now I'm older.

Rachael Fenlon (10)
St Basil's Primary School, Widnes

THE SUBJECT OF THIS POEM IS . . .

As long as an elastic band,
As fast as a flea,
As smooth as a teddy bear,
As clever as can be.

As smelly as a pig's breath,
As noisy as a drum,
As playful as a jack-in-the-box,
As annoying as a hum.

As fat as a hippo,
As greedy as can be,
As friendly as a cat,
As soft as a mushy pea.

What is it?

Michael Corrigan (8)
St Basil's Primary School, Widnes

THE SUBJECT OF THIS POEM IS . . .

As small as a twig,
As green as grass,
As spiky as a thorn,
As hairy as a bear,
As greedy as a pig,
As slow as a tortoise,
As clever as a magician,
As fat as a cat,
As good as gold,
As smelly as a baby.

What is it?

Jamie Sanderson (9)
St Basil's Primary School, Widnes

THE OBJECT OF THIS POEM IS . . .

As smelly as a pig
As fat as a hippo's belly
As furry as a gentleman's wig
As slimy as jelly

As long as a python
As grey as a storm cloud
As slow as a snail
As noisy as a crowd

As muddy as a pig
As rough as a rock
As tall as a tree
As loud as a cock

What is it?

Leah Barton (9)
St Basil's Primary School, Widnes

A GIANT MYTHICAL MONSTER

A mythical monster lives in a land far away,
His cheeks are redder than a baby's cheeks,
He is greener than a bear,
He is happier than a clown,
His eyes are rounder than a ball,
His legs are thicker than a tree trunk,
His nose is bigger than a bus,
He is uglier than a snail,
He is grumpier than a crocodile,
His claws are sharper than a cat's.

Ellie Ogburn (8)
St Basil's Primary School, Widnes

A Storm At Sea

As we struggled through the ocean
The winds blew a gale,
We rowed and rowed
But still we came to fail.

Lightning struck, thunder roared,
My boat rocked from side to side,
Dodging and passing the furious waves,
The sea a never-ending slide.

I was scared, what should I do?
The waves were getting taller,
I'm getting splashed, I'm getting soaked,
My ship is getting smaller.

Then calm, the storm at last has gone,
Peaceful is the sea,
I look around to find my friends,
To realise there's only me.

Michelle Stead (11)
St Basil's Primary School, Widnes

Year Six

Oh no it's the year of doom,
Year six, I don't want to go.
It's too hard,
Extra homework in year five,
I think that would do.

Then again there's the Conway Centre,
Camelot at the end of the year,
But what about leaving?
I don't want to leave.

Today's the day I go to year six,
I'm in my new line.
Hey this isn't so bad,
It's not that hard,
I think I'll like this year after all.

Claire Smith (11)
St Basil's Primary School, Widnes

HALLOWE'EN NIGHT

One spooky night when the stars were bright
A witch came up to me
All dressed in black, with a pumpkin light
She invited me for tea

She took me to her slimy black house
It smelt like she was cooking an old trout
I saw a cauldron on the fire
Then the flames go higher and higher

She went to make a slimy potion
I was very scared, but showed no emotion
If she thought I was going to drink that
She had another thing coming
The silly old bat

In she hobbled with a glint in her eye
Here you are dear, have a try
I threw the glass and ran as fast as I could,
Straight through the house and back through the wood

I woke up frightened, I was lying in my bed
A Hallowe'en dream, all in my head.

Jessica Forshaw (9)
St Basil's Primary School, Widnes

DIFFERENT SEASONS

Spring

Spring, spring what a good thing.
Flowers grow in the spring,
Daffodils, roses, lilies,
All blossom from their stem.

Summer

Summer, summer what a good thing,
Brings the sun and makes it clean,
Swimming pools out,
Fans on and up and about.

Autumn

Autumn, autumn what a bad thing,
All the leaves fall off the trees.
Wrapping up warm,
I like the colours of the leaves.

Winter

Winter, winter what a bad and good thing,
Snowmen built,
Coats on, hats and scarf,
But fingers and toes totally froze.

Sophie Deegan (10)
St Basil's Primary School, Widnes

A NEW BEGINNING

Spring

> Spring starts the year
> With warm beginnings,
> The flowers start to grow,
> Out come the bumblebees.

Summer

> Hot summer burning us,
> Sun's out, suncream on,
> On the beach, in the pool,
> It's summer everywhere

Autumn

> The leaves begin to turn golden brown,
> They start to fall,
> Conkers bombard on people's heads,
> I start to collect them all like a squirrel.

Winter

> In comes the snow,
> Out come the children.
> Here comes the snowmen,
> Ahhh a cold snowball slides down my top.

Craig Gifford (10)
St Basil's Primary School, Widnes

THE READER OF THIS POEM IS . . .

The reader of this poem is . . .
As thick as a brick,
As cheeky as a baby's lick,
As sad as a boy,
As squeaky as a toy.

As smelly as a welly,
As wobbly as a jelly,
As dirty as dishwater,
As dumb as a daughter.

As hairy as a cat,
As blind as a bat,
As funny as a hyena,
As chatty as Tina.

As naughty as a rat,
As tall as a top hat,
As sharp as a pencil,
As neat as a stencil.

Emma Hunt (11)
St Basil's Primary School, Widnes

THE OBJECT OF THIS POEM IS . . .

As hairy as a sheep,
As quick as lightning,
As scary as a ghost,
As small as a pea.

As prickly as a hedgehog,
As ugly as a bat,
As sharp as a knife,
As black as coal,
As light as a feather.

As tricky as a sum,
As warm as a mug of tea,
As quick as a mouse,
As clever as a scientist,
As hungry as a lion.

What is it?

Suzanna Hughes (9)
St Basil's Primary School, Widnes

NIGHT SOUNDS

When I go upstairs to bed I hear . . .
My mum creeping up the stairs,
My dad slamming the doors,
The cars speeding down the street.

Half asleep
And half awake,
My mum shouting on the phone,
The rain bashing,
The wind crying,
The aeroplane roaring.

Half asleep
And half awake,
The cat purring,
The dog barking,
The fish singing,
The pig jumping,
The bird swimming.

Then I hear nothing - nothing at all
Because I'm asleep, sound asleep.

Jennifer Fisher (9)
St Basil's Primary School, Widnes

A NEW SISTER

I was happy when my baby sister was born,
Everyone was jumping for joy.
Waiting for her to be born,
A start of a new beginning,
Happy families,
We were looking forward to starting again.
Screaming, crying,
Going in the cupboards, eating the sponge in the bath,
Splashing, splashing,
Getting on our nerves.
Eating something dangerous,
All scrapes, scares and scratches.
Drinking all the milk, crying for some tea,
Screaming, she's been stung by a bumblebee.
Digging her sharp nails into me,
Pulling my sweet hair,
Playing boo, making her cry.
Watching Big Brother,
Screaming all the way through.
Watching the last series,
Falling asleep in my arms.
She makes me feel like a mum,
Put her to bed.
Phew, fast asleep,
Nice and quiet now,
No more screaming.

Megan Prendergast (10)
St Basil's Primary School, Widnes

A NEW BEGINNING

I felt really scared when I started school,
I was left in the playground,
People were staring at me,
Playing in that large playground on my own,
Thinking what do I know about all these worrying rules?

Went into school on my first day,
I met a new friend called May.
My first teacher was Miss Darcy,
All my friends were gathered around.
I was so worried about the new year,
My teacher said, 'Don't you worry dear.'

The bell rings time for play,
So many lunatics screaming their heads off,
So I tried to get attention so I coughed my head off,
Went into the playhouse in my class,
I decided to share the toys,
Then I realised the day weren't so bad.

In the middle of the day
There was something that was really funny,
My best friend called May said she was a queen.
At the end of the day I didn't want to leave my class,
She made my new school a blast,
I loved it in reception.

Jennifer Shard (10)
St Basil's Primary School, Widnes

MY MORNING

Yawn, yawn,
Get out of bed,
Come on get up,
Sleepy head.

Down the stairs,
Eat your toast,
Drink your milk,
Get the post.

Brush your teeth,
Wash your face,
Put on your clothes,
Tie your lace.

Pick up your bag,
Go out the door,
Off to school
To work some more.

Rebecca Gray (11)
St Basil's Primary School, Widnes

MY VOYAGE

My life is like a voyage,
I'm sailing on the sea,
Sometimes crashing over rocks
Which makes me feel as unhappy as can be.

My life is like a voyage,
I'm sailing on the sea,
Breathing the fresh, calm air,
Surely this makes me happy.

My life is like a voyage,
I'm sailing on the sea,
I have to continue my journey
Although I have nowhere to go,
So goodbye for now,
I have to go now, some way, somehow.

Dean Abdy (11)
St Basil's Primary School, Widnes

DRINKS

Coca Cola is very fizzy,
Take a little sip
And it will make you go
Totally dizzy.

Milkshakes make loads of bubbles
But once they pop you'll
Have lots of
Little puddles!

Loads of men
Have loads of beer,
But once they've finished
They cannot steer.

Fanta has a lovely taste,
It's a drink
You definitely would not
Want to waste.

Tea tastes nice and sweet,
Once you've finished
the cup you'll feel
Really neat.

Jake Baker (11)
St Basil's Primary School, Widnes

THE WITCH

There was a witch
Who lived in a ditch,
She wanted to make a potion
But she wouldn't tell anyone about the special lotion.

The things she put in were,
A tin, half a newt,
And a stinky, dirty boot.

A poor pussy cat,
And a dirty old mat,
And a smelly old rat.

She got her broom,
And vanished with a *boom!*
She landed in a little boy's room.

She put the lotion on his table, and said,
'Sticky rats, smelly old mats
Take me back to the ditch and my cats.'

Charlotte Cunningham (11)
St Basil's Primary School, Widnes

FIREWORKS

There is a whirlwind in my garden
Shooting colours bright,
Shooting out its blooms
To fade quietly in the night.

There was an explosion over my head
Where the thunder roared a name,
To shoot the plumes of colour
So down to Earth they came.

There's an arrow in my garden,
It's waiting patiently
'Til it's allowed to fly,
Where no man can be.

There's a bomb in my garden,
The fuse sprays colours so bright,
And when the fuse is at the end,
Bang! Will end the colours of the night.

Sam Ainsworth (10)
St Basil's Primary School, Widnes

THE READER OF THIS POEM IS . . .

The reader of this poem is . . .
As large as a tree,
As weird as me,
And as old as a granny.

The reader of this poem is . . .
As dumb as a dog,
As mad as a hatter,
And as dull as fog.

The reader of this poem is . . .
As quick as a lick,
As horrible as a witch,
And as thin as a stick.

The reader of this poem is . . .
As blind as a bat,
As white as Snow White,
As brainy as a cat,
And as dodgy as a Jammy Dodger.

Of course it would have to be you!

Carla Douglas (11)
St Basil's Primary School, Widnes

MY ENEMY SCOTT

My enemy Scott
Is absolutely crazy,
But in his house
He's really lazy.

My enemy Scott
Says he's super strong,
I don't believe him
And his feet really pong.

My enemy Scott
Thinks he's really fast,
But in any race
He'll always come last.

My enemy Scott
Has a friend called Mick,
He's really slow
And super thick.

My enemy Scott
Has a huge bald head,
He's that brave and courageous
He takes his teddy to bed.

Shaun Morris (10)
St Basil's Primary School, Widnes

ANGER IS . . .

Anger is listening to my sister shouting.
Anger is when my sister barges into my bedroom.
Anger is getting grounded.
Anger is when I have to hurry in school.

Kevin Hunt (8)
St Basil's Primary School, Widnes

FIREWORKS

There is a whirlwind in my garden
Spraying colours bright,
Shooting out its blooms
To quietly fade in the night.

There was an explosion over my head
Where the thunder made itself king,
To shoot the plumes of colour
The Catherine wheel sings.

It's ready for lift-off
On the count of three,
It shoots up in the air
Where everyone can see.

Daniel Rowlands (10)
St Basil's Primary School, Widnes

IN EMMA'S BEDROOM

There were . . .
Ten oinking pigs on my bed,
Nine big ponies galloping all around,
Eight crocodiles snapping at me,
Seven birds tweeting all the time,
Six parrots squawking under my bed,
Five dogs barking on my bed,
Four rabbits eating all the time,
Three hamsters tutting everywhere,
Two fish swimming around,
One - why do I have to live here?

Emma Parker (8)
St Basil's Primary School, Widnes

THE WRITER OF THIS POEM

The writer of this poem
Is as pretty as a picture,
As clever as a calculator,
As strong as Superman.

As helpful as a barmaid,
As busy as a bee,
As loud as an ogre's footsteps,
As funny as a clown.

As slow as a grandma,
As crazy as a baboon,
As thin as a pencil.

As light as a feather,
As strict as ten nuns,
As groovy as a gorilla.

Cara Richardson (9)
St Basil's Primary School, Widnes

THE ZUNICORN

This monster is . . .
Bigger than a block of flats,
More bendy than an elastic band,
Faster than a racing car,
Stronger than a human hand.

Wider than a big palace,
He is scared of being up high,
Fatter than an elephant,
He always takes a big sigh.

Greedier than a big giant,
More wrinkly than an old granny,
His footsteps as quiet as can be,
Longer than your biggest nanny.

Joanne Hughes (8)
St Basil's Primary School, Widnes

THE BLIZZARD

There was a blizzard outside,
I was in the snow,
I couldn't find the door,
There was no way to go.

It was the middle of the night,
It was getting cold,
I was still digging
Until I saw a light.

It was a bluish green,
Going brighter, brighter,
Then I saw that fateful beam.

I heard a bing, I heard a bong,
It was a snow machine going wrong.

It cleared off the snow,
The adventure was over,
I found a way out,
It was definitely over.

Daniel Barlow (9)
St Basil's Primary School, Widnes

LAZY BONES

Get out of bed,
Don't be a fool,
Look at the time,
You'll be late for school.

Eat your breakfast,
Hurry up,
Wash your face
You mucky pup.

Get on the playground,
Don't delay,
The sooner we're finished,
We can go and play.

Get into bed,
Turn off your light,
Shut your door,
And say goodnight.

Angela Hill (11)
St Basil's Primary School, Widnes

STARS

As bright as the sun,
As pretty as can be,
Colours as bright as a bumblebee.
They light our way
When we cannot see,
They always smile along with me.

They make me smile,
They make me sing,
And that is why I love to be king.

Can it be true, do they love you?
No one knows but I certainly do,
I watch them at night,
But I don't fly a kite,
I just sleep till morning is bright.

Samantha Howard (10)
St Basil's Primary School, Widnes

THE WITCH

There was once a witch
Who had an itch,
One day she was casting a spell
Which went very well.

The witch added loads
Of slimy, horrible toads,
And added some snails,
And also cats' nails.

She lit a candle in the pumpkin,
When it burnt out she put it in the bin,
The witch lived on top of a mountain,
And on the house was a lantern.

On every Hallowe'en
I always hear a scream,
The witch takes her broom,
And said, 'I'll be back soon.'

She made a curse
Which became worse,
People thought she was creepy,
And this made everyone weepy.

Susan Bates (11)
St Basil's Primary School, Widnes

SUPER SIMILES

The object of this poem is . . .
As boring as the news,
As still as a box,
As smooth as a snake.

As hard as nails,
As colourful as a picture,
As messy as my tray,
As shiny as steel.

As bright as the sun,
As round as the Earth,
As deep as the well.

What is it?

Sam Filkins (8)
St Basil's Primary School, Widnes

IT'S HALLOWE'EN TIME

It's icy cold, it's really dark,
And I'm stuck here in the park.
I came to play, I went to hide,
But somehow I got locked inside.

It's the witching hour, it's Hallowe'en,
I'm really spooked by what I've seen.
It was nasty and green, not dull but bright,
With huge hairy legs, it gave me a fright.

Maybe it's a ghoul with no fingers and toes
Or it might be a witch with a long pointed nose.
It's coming towards me, could it be the Grim Reaper?
I sigh with relief it's just the park keeper.

Karl Pierce (9)
St Basil's Primary School, Widnes

NONSENSE RHYMES

The breeze made the man freeze,
Which made him sneeze,
Which blew down the trees,
And he scared the bees.

The mouse in the house
Kept saying please,
For some tasty cheese,
Which made him wheeze.

The horse jumped over the house
On a spoon to the moon,
And found a balloon,
Then got shot by a harpoon.

Dominic Naylor (10)
St Basil's Primary School, Widnes

HAPPINESS IS . . .

Happiness is getting a new bike.
Happiness is getting a new scooter for my birthday.
Happiness is getting new shoes.
Happiness is going to the Wacky Warehouse.
Happiness is moving house.

Daniel Steadman (8)
St Basil's Primary School, Widnes

THE ZEGRUB

This monster is . . .

More terrifying than a zombie that has risen from Hell,
Heavier than ninety-nine alligators lying on each other,
More intelligent than Frankenstein's mother,
More wrinkly than an old granny picking her spots,
Bigger than a flying dinosaur zooming as high as it can,
Fatter than King Henry VIII when he was beheading people,
Scarier than a tarantula attacking you on the belly,
Hairier than a gorilla scratching its bum.

Sophia Riccio (9)
St Basil's Primary School, Widnes

HAPPY BIRTHDAY MOON

I will give you,
A red balloon to float you into space,
A yellow sun so you can see in the dark,
A green blanket to keep you warm,
A silver flag to show you're you,
A blue fish to give you company,
A black and white star just for fun,
A grey bed for you to sleep in,
A gold teddy for you to cuddle.

Alice Young (8)
St James' CE Primary School, Audlem

THE PIED PIPER

The Pied Piper stepped into the street,
Walking into the town centre.
As he gripped his long varnished pipe with his hand
He blew the first note,
The next thing you could hear was a small mumbling -
Growing to a loud grumbling,
A mighty rumbling.
Out came the rats fumbling and tumbling,
Bumping, jumping, rushing and pushing,
Flashing and dashing and splashing
Into the river's water deep and wide,
Washing the walls on the southern side,
                                    Silence.

Craig Hughes (11)
St James' CE Primary School, Audlem

THE IRON MAN

I   ron man.
R   ound his ears the wind swirled.
O   n top of the cliff the iron man stood.
N   ever before had the iron man seen the sea.

M   agnificent head turned left, then right.
A   seagull perched on the iron man's shoulder.
N   o one knows where the iron man had come from.

Katherine Morley (8)
St James' CE Primary School, Audlem

THE THING

There were paw marks in the sand,
They looked like a human hand.

There was a quiet sort of sound
That was like a hovering cloud.

I thought it was a prowling cat
Or it could be a flying bat.

It was then that I found
Something that sounded very loud.

I walked back to land
And found it was a band.

They were playing a song
That went on too long!

Joshua Niblett (9)
St John's CE Aided Primary School, Sandbach

THE THING

The Thing - it lives in a jungle far away.
The Thing - is a horrible, smelly creature.
He can scare you but when people scare him he will still stay.
You can't see the Thing but wherever you are he will be following.
No one knows what the Thing looks like,
He is invisible.
People run away because they can smell him.
He isn't vicious.
He eats lots of fruit
But he will eat humans instead.
Sometimes he will scare you like this . . . *roar!*

Max Davenport (9)
St John's CE Aided Primary School, Sandbach

I WAS A TREE

I was a tree . . .

There is a bumblebee
Going to its hive
In the middle of the wood
In my leaves.

A scurrying of ants,
The buzzing of bees
Is sounding in my ears.

My leaves are brown and falling,
I soon will be bare,
It happens every year.

Now my life is at an end,
I can't be a woodcutter's friend,
The last tree in front of me is gone.

Here comes the woodcutter!
I am going to die!

Matthew King (8)
St John's CE Aided Primary School, Sandbach

I WANT TO BE THUMPER, MY RABBIT

I want to be Thumper, my rabbit
Because you don't do much,
You just laze about,
You rely on the humans to feed you,
To give you water,
To clean you out,
That's why I want to be Thumper, my rabbit.

Samantha Proudlove (9)
St John's CE Aided Primary School, Sandbach

I WISH I WAS A RALLY DRIVER

I wish I was a rally driver
Speeding round the track.

I wish that my co-driver
Wasn't called Jack.

I wish I could drive a Toyota
With its really powerful motor.

There would be powerful crashes
With lots of loud bashes.

Driving up to one fifty miles per hour,
Sweating heavily every hour.

At the end of the day
I park my car in its bay.

Then I have a cup of tea
As I dream of what I would like to be.

Michael Wellings (9)
St John's CE Aided Primary School, Sandbach

AUTUMN

Golden the bracken,
Crunchy the leaves,
Smell of a bonfire carried by a breeze,
Touch of frost makes cold my ears,
Taste of blackberries,
Autumn is here!

Cassy Lawton-Jenkins (9)
St John's CE Aided Primary School, Sandbach

How Good It Is To Be A Mouse

If I were a mouse
I could run so fast,
I could twitch my nose.

I would be a lovely pet,
I would have a mousehole,
I could have big white ears.

I would be fluffy,
I would be able to have white teeth,
I would be eating cheese.

I wouldn't go to school,
I would be able to squeak,
I wouldn't be able to laugh.

I wouldn't be able to talk,
I wouldn't be able to shout,
I would run around in circles.

Thomas Faulkner (9)
St John's CE Aided Primary School, Sandbach

Why Do We Have . . . ?

Why do we have the sea rising on land?
Why do we have strong winds blowing upon the land?
Why do we have lots of rain falling round here?
Why do we not have rain on the plains when we need it?
Why do we not have strong winds on the plains when we need them?

Rory Schurer-Lewis (8)
St John's CE Aided Primary School, Sandbach

I Wish I Was A White Tiger

If I were a white tiger
I would prowl around.

If I were a white tiger
I would run around.

If I were a white tiger
I would stalk my prey.

If I were a white tiger
I would roar and say,
'Get off my prey!'

And the blood would pour
All over my fur,
And I would let it dry.

Anna White (9)
St John's CE Aided Primary School, Sandbach

I Dream

The dream that I was dreaming
Was that I wanted legs like a cheetah.

You ask me why I wanted legs like a cheetah.
To move fast.

You ask me why I wanted to move fast.
To catch my prey.

You ask me why I want to catch my prey.
To eat it.

You ask me why I want to eat my prey.
Because I am hungry.

You ask me why I am hungry.
I haven't eaten for a week!

Zachariah Shaikh (8)
St John's CE Aided Primary School, Sandbach

THIS IS THE CHIMNEY THAT SANTA NEEDS TO GO DOWN!

This is the room that Santa needs,
And this is the chimney that Santa needs to go down.
This is the reindeer who's blocking the chimney that
Santa needs to go down.

These are the children who are watching the reindeer
Who's blocking the chimney that Santa needs to go down.
These are the parents who have come down and seen the
Children watching the reindeer who's blocking the
Chimney that Santa needs to go down.

These are the streetlights that have just come on, and
These are the neighbours yelling 'What's the racket?'
The racket is the parents who have come down and seen
The children who are watching the reindeer who is
Blocking the chimney which Santa needs to go down.

And this is the morning where all is quiet, and here is the
Chimney that Santa needed once, but not any more,
Because when the family were in bed,
That cheeky Santa he used the door.

Heidi Wood (10)
St John's CE Aided Primary School, Bollington

13 THINGS TO DO WITH A JUMPER

They gave me a jumper that was jade green
The first thing I wanted to do was scream!

As a scarf I wear it around my neck
Teachers say 'Stop that!' I say 'What the heck!'

I've a St John's uniform, all smart and new
And when I'm hungry I can give it a chew.

When it's a nibble I need but can find no tuck
I'll grab a sleeve and give it a good suck.

On boring rainy days inside the hall
I have loads of fun and roll it up as a ball.

A pillow it makes when stuffed with socks
Dangled on string I have a good box.

Sometimes when feeling like a little mole
I get part of a cuff and burrow through a hole.

Playtime in the park on a wee slide
Under my bum, it makes a great mat to glide.

I could use it as a blanket if only I had a cat
Instead I'll stick it on my head and wear it as a hat.

To carry it around is one big chore
Tied around my waist as a belt, it's less of a bore!

A stretch and a roll, I can have a skip
Tied to some chair legs someone will trip.

Oh yes, the days I'm cold I wear it over a shirt,
If I was a girl it could become a skirt.

As it gets old and Mum says 'It's a rag'
I'll give it to the school and they can use it as a flag.

James Flood
St John's CE Aided Primary School, Bollington

THE FALCON

A falcon's eyes are full of wonder,
He can be as nasty as thunder,
That's what will happen if you make a blunder.

His wings are very wide and long,
He squawks and shouts 'cause that's his song,
He has a beak that's sharp and strong.

Anthony McMullin (9)
St Michael's RC Primary School, Widnes

WINNIE THE POOH

Winnie was walking around the wood,
Searching for as much honey as he could,
When he fell down a hill and landed in mud.

Hungry and dirty was Winnie The Pooh
He didn't know what to do.
So he cleaned himself up and had some stew.

Vanessa Briggs (8)
St Michael's RC Primary School, Widnes

SUMMER DAYS

The summer days are far away
When I can go out to play
I think of sunny days by the sea
Places like these, I long to be.

Jennifer Golson (8)
St Michael's RC Primary School, Widnes

THE MAN WITH A BIG NOSE

There was a man who had a big nose
It was so big it nearly touched his toes
And every day it grows and grows.

He walked down to the park
When it was very very dark
And there he saw a little lark.

Ryan Grimes (9)
St Michael's RC Primary School, Widnes

THE WIND

The wind is whistling down my ear
It's dark and cold but I don't fear
The whistling wind is all I hear.

Even though I should be in bed
Wrapped up warm with my ted
The whistling wind still rushes round my head.

Samantha McCarthy (9)
St Michael's RC Primary School, Widnes

FOOTBALL

Football
Some footballs are big, some footballs are small
To win you have to score a goal.
Sometimes players go to the Mall
Manchester's striker is Andy Cole.

Some of the players are very tall,
Vicky gives David Beckham a call,
One of the players falls over the wall.

Even in the pouring rain
Teams always have to train,
And their feet get sore after kicking the ball.

Josh McGiveron (9)
St Michael's RC Primary School, Widnes

MAD MRS MURREY

Mad Mrs Murrey
Is always in a hurry
Bouncing here and bouncing there
She is such a worry.
Although so sincere
She always stinks of curry,
I think she comes from Bury
Her husband drives a lorry,
Cattle is his main load.
To take to market to be sold.
Then back home to his wife Kerry.

Amy Bredin (8)
St Michael's RC Primary School, Widnes

A MOTHER'S JOY

There once was a little boy
Who brought his mum a lot of joy,
He played a lot with his wooden toy.
He helped his mum around the house
And even caught a mouse.
His friends at school think he's cool
But sometimes he plays the fool.

Joshua Craig (8)
St Michael's RC Primary School, Widnes

FLAMES OF THE WIND

I dragged Beauty from the Earth
and flung it into the misty air.
I jogged after the puffed clouds as they flew
across the sapphire sky.
I walked towards Enjoyment and grabbed
Bravery in gloved hands.
I pushed Embarrassment for a breezy slide
down the concrete path.
I stopped Anxiety at the grassy roadside
and threw it towards Luck.
I snapped Ugliness in half
I sprinted past Love and kept going
till sleepy of that squealing noise.
I sat down for a short break at the door of Hope.

Claire Bolger (11)
Winsford High Street Primary School

THE WILD RABBIT

A rabbit comes out early in the morning,
Starts its day by eating veg
By eleven o'clock he goes and explores
Shades of blue and shades of red.
Splashes in the pond and talks to the birds
The bark on the trees looks like a werewolf.

A rabbit is cute, cute as a teddy
With a cute little smile and very very steady
The trees on the leaves, green as grass.

Hopping around all day long
Licking the water in the pond.
Then hops home for his bath
Soon he's home, walking up the path.

Lucy Rowsell (10)
Winsford High Street Primary School

THE SEA AND BEACH

I can see people swimming in the sea
I look at the people,
And see a fish nibbling
In the sea.
I can see papers on the sea
Brown, grey, yellow, blue and green.
I can see shells in the sea
I can hear the sea crashing on the rocks.
I can smell the salt in the sea
And the hot-dogs sizzling.
I can see the sea pushing the
Shells on the beach.
Also children playing in the sea
Jumping over waves.
But also I can see
Fish living happily in the deep blue sea.
Making a friend when they nibble
On people's knees.
I can see fish living happily
In the deep blue sea.
Dolphins swimming
In the deep blue sea.

Holly May Holmes (9)
Winsford High Street Primary School

WALKING THROUGH THE PARK

As I walk through the park
Even though it's nearly dark,
As I see sweet wrappers
As I think there are kidnappers
As I hear twigs cracking
Now I hear a dog yapping
As I see big trees
Now I shiver down to my knees
And there's a shop that I've never seen
A place where I've never been
As I walk up to it
All I see is a light lit
As I touch all the walls
As I walk in the halls
As I walk out
I have a look about
As I smell all the flowers
As I walk for hours and hours
As I walk on the path
Then there was an enormous laugh
As I wonder where it's coming from
Oh, it's him, my mate Tom
He and I walk to school together
We could be friends for ever and ever
Now it's time to go home
As we walk home alone, alone.

Justin Rolfe (10)
Winsford High Street Primary School

THE SHOPPING CENTRE

When I walk into the shopping centre
A thousand noises hit my ears
Children shouting, babies screaming
Shopkeepers 'Yes, please!'
Everyone moving from shop to shop
As I walk past the chip shop
I get the smell of chips cooking
A child runs and trips
A baby starts screaming throughout the shopping centre
The shopping centre is as loud as a pack of wolves
And as full as a school of children
Children are mithering for sweets
As I walk out the shopping centre
Noises fade away until I come to the shopping centre
On another day.

Stephanie Turner (9)
Winsford High Street Primary School

BIRTHDAYS

I feel happy opening my presents
Saying 'I've got £35 from the cards.'
Opening presents, saying 'I've always wanted that, thank you.'
Blowing out my ten candles
Eating my cake is the best, jam sponge with icing. I love parties.
Having a disco, friends come dancing all night through.
In the morning I am tired because of
All the dancing I did.

Karis Bell (10)
Winsford High Street Primary School

SCHOOL

I get into school and see children talking
Teacher calls the register,
Everyone's rushing through the halls to assembly
When we get there children talk,
Teacher tells everyone to be quiet.
She tells a story about the creation
I think she's on a diet.

When assembly is over we go back to class
Our teacher tells us what to do,
I think everyone would rather throw their books,
Rustling of paper all around,
I can't wait till we're in the playground
In the playground, I have lots of fun
I'm glad that my English work's done.

Back in class, maths is easy
At lunchtime I can smell all the food in the hall,
In class again, it's time for art,
After art we get our homework,
Then we go home, I'm really glad.

Daniel Knight (10)
Winsford High Street Primary School

FLOWERS

Flowers grow from under the ground,
Bluebells ring and make peaceful sounds.
Tulips are being picked
Rose stems are letting people, be pricked.

People make daisies into chains,
But more grow back when it rains.
Flowers let out scents that attract bees,
They eat from the sun by letting
Out their leaves.

Flowers are different
Some catch flies
Flying around the flowers are butterflies.

Louis Lumsden (9)
Winsford High Street Primary School

THE OLD BUILDING

An old building
Is boarded up
Spooky, terrifying and broken
It's like a field with nobody there,
Like a lonely town
It makes me feel scary
An old building.

Lauren Gelsthorpe (10)
Winsford High Street Primary School

SEEING IN THE CITY

I can see people in the city
being noisy everywhere.
I can see people walking into pubs and clubs
I can smell aftershave from people as they walk
                              past in the streets.
I can see in the city, things that happen and go on.
In the city I can hear and see people winning money,
the sound of money falling from the machines.
I can feel people knocking their arms against
                              others as they walk past.
I can see people enjoyment burgers,
I wish I had one too.

Steven Briggs (9)
Winsford High Street Primary School

SEASONS

Seasons of the year are
Spring, summer
Autumn, winter.
In the spring bluebells grow,
The farmer plants seeds too.
A scarecrow is up to scare the crows.
It's summer, time to play
The kids cool themselves down,
Fathers say 'Let's have a BBQ today!'
When it's autumn, the leaves turn brown
They also turn gold,
The colour of the Queen's crown.
Well it's winter, with snow on the ground
On Christmas Eve, Rudolf
And Santa fly around.

Naomi Hurst (9)
Winsford High Street Primary School

ANIMALS

I went to see the animals
And what a sight it was.
Monkeys, tigers, bats and owls,
Monkeys laugh, tigers growl.

Elephants were slow and steady,
Squirting water, let's get ready.
Tigers growling, elephants showering.
The bats are black, monkeys hiding in a sack
And monkeys swing from tree to tree.

I went to see the animals
And what a sight it was,
Monkeys, tigers, bats and owls,
Monkeys laugh, tigers growl.

Danielle Grindrod (10)
Winsford High Street Primary School

SEASONS

Spring is where the buds come out,
People are out and about,
Green grass grows,
All different shades
The sky is going blue,
As dark as the deep blue sea.
Whilst the sun is coming through
Her comes summer.
Roasting hot,
No babies are in their cots.
Sunbathing is for everybody
Perfume of red roses.
Animals are out playing about,
Birds are tweeting
Ice-pops melting.
Time to get the paddling pool out,
Summer is vanishing into autumn!
Autumn is here with brown crunchy leaves,
Dancing and prancing around.
No fun of summer now, no time for ice,
No time for the pool.
Winter is here now, snow hiding the land,
Like a white fleece blanket,
Throwing and chucking snowballs round and round.

Sarah Nixon (9)
Winsford High Street Primary School

THE BEACH

On the beach lies golden sand
I get some in my hand
And it also covers the land.

The fragrance of fresh air and ice cream
Makes the beach a beautiful scene
The boiling hot sun
Makes it lots of fun.

The sound of children in my ears
'Hey Dad, over here!'

On the beach lies golden sand
I get some in my hand
And it covers the land.

The sky turns grey
So let's pack away
And leave the bay.

There's blue carpet in the house
Now off to feed my pet mouse!

Adam Broadley (9)
Winsford High Street Primary School

WINTER

The daylight was fading away
The stormy knight was coming
The clouds were going black
The snow started falling
The howling, whistling wind
The meowing wind went louder.

The crashing thundering
The flashing lightning

The sky was dark and gloomy
The wind went badder and madder
The kids' noses went red
Now it's time to go to bed.

Olivia Bywater (10)
Winsford High Street Primary School

IN THE WOODS

Branches on the trees brushing
Against my face
Trees swaying, acorns falling
Birds fluttering, bees buzzing
Spiders are running away
Leaves like hedgehogs scurrying along

Dogs swimming in the lake
Children climbing trees
Leaves crunching under your feet
Rain smacking against the leaves
The rain started to fall
About an hour later
The sun came out
From behind the rain clouds

In summer the trees will be green
The trees will be swaying in the breeze.

Nick Wilcock (10)
Winsford High Street Primary School

SUMMERTIME

As I walk into the park
I feel a breeze upon my face.

I bought a burger, it's a bit of a con
It almost cost me £1.71.

Over there, twigs are cracking
There are some birds overhead
With their wings flapping.

I walk past a bush, it skims my face,
And I sit on bench to tie my lace.

I sit near a pond that glitters in the light
There are some children flying a kite.

The trees in the park, tower over me,
This park is such a beautiful sight to see.

I can see people eating their lunch,
With them I think they brought punch.

Now it is becoming night
I really wish it was still light.

I have to walk through the town to get home,
And because it is late, I am all alone.

I have just been to the park and I'm nearly home,
When I get in my dog will bark and my brothers will moan.

Daniel Gilmore (10)
Winsford High Street Primary School

CHRISTMAS AND NEW YEAR

On Christmas Eve I get very excited
I went to bed very early.
I left a pie and milk for Santa
And a carrot for Rudolf.
On Christmas Day I open my presents
I get teddies, games and toys.
I go out for tea
I have turkey and roast potatoes
I see Santa everywhere
I see him in shops, on cards and on wrapping paper
I love Christmas.

I love the New Year party
At the end of the year
Dancing all night long
My New Year's resolution is to be more friendly.

Happy New Year
Girls and boys!

Chelsea Struthers (10)
Winsford High Street Primary School

SNAKE

A snake
It has no legs
It has scaly skin, looks funny and can be slimy
It is like slime running through your fingers
It is like a worm sliding through the grass
It makes me feel big
Big like a giant
A snake

Catherine Ann Luckett (10)
Winsford High Street Primary School

WHAT ANIMALS DO

I can see dogs wagging tails
I can see birds flying
I can see pigs playing in the mud
I can hear dogs barking
I can hear pigs oinking
I can hear birds tweeting
I can hear cats miaowing
I can hear lions roaring
I can see humans with a lead and on
The other end is a doggy
I can see people stroking a dog
And saying its name
So I want another go, again, again, again.
I can hear people say 'Don't touch that!
It's got prickles.'

Jennifer Jenkins (9)
Winsford High Street Primary School

WINTER

The snow was arriving
The clouds were dying
The wind let out a sudden howl
Snow appears on the ground
Everything was white it was coming bright
Snowflakes fell to the ground
I can hear the wind
I can hear the trees
I can hear myself speak.

Holly Wohlleben (9)
Winsford High Street Primary School

THE SPIDER

There are lots of spiders
Some even have red knees
The spiders will live anywhere
They'll even live in trees!

There are many kinds of spiders
These are just a few,
Tarantula, red kneed and funnel-web
Black widow too!

There is another spider
Called the redback
They're especially good at hunting
And working in a pack.

If spiders could enter an art contest
They would surely win
All the time they spend on it
How neatly they can spin.

A web is a masterpiece of art
A spider is clever and really smart.

Jonathon Armstrong (10)
Winsford High Street Primary School

FOG IS

Fog is like smoke from a fire drifting through the air
It is a curtain, a blanket covering the ground
It is almost like see-through snow
It is a black cloud of the night
Fog is like chalk dust
Fog is

Jessica Buchan (11)
Winsford High Street Primary School